# A PRACTICAL GUIDE
# TO RESEARCH AND SERVICE
# WITH HIDDEN POPULATIONS

Edited by

## Stephanie Tortu
*School of Public Health and Tropical Medicine*
*Tulane University*

## Lloyd A. Goldsamt
*National Development and Research Institutes, Inc.*

## Rahul Hamid
*National Development and Research Institutes, Inc.*

**Allyn and Bacon**

Boston • London • Toronto • Sydney • Tokyo • Singapore

*Executive editor:*   Rebecca Pascal
*Manufacturing buyer:*   JoAnne Sweeney
*Senior marketing manager:*   Caroline Croley
*Cover designer:*   hannusdesign.com
*Production coordinator:*   Pat Torelli Publishing Services
*Editorial-production service:*   Stratford Publishing Services, Inc.
*Electronic composition:*   Stratford Publishing Services, Inc.

Copyright © 2002 by Allyn & Bacon
A Pearson Education Company
75 Arlington Street
Boston, MA 02116

Internet: www.ablongman.com

**Library of Congress Cataloging-in-Publication Data**

A practical guide to research and service with hidden populations / edited by Stephanie
Tortu, Lloyd A. Goldsamt, Rahul Hamid.

    p.     cm.
    Includes bibliographical references and index.
    ISBN 0-205-27488-9
    1. Marginality, social—Research—United States—Methodology.   2. Human
services—United States.   I. Tortu, Stephanie.   II. Goldsamt, Lloyd A.   III. Hamid,
Rahul.

HN90.M26 P73 2002
305.5'6'0723—dc21

                                          200102243

Printed in the United States of America
10 9 8 7 6 5 4 3 2 1   RRD-VA   05 04 03 02 01

# CONTENTS

# FOREWORD

This book comes at a critical time in public health and social science research, when significant strides have been made in the delivery of a range of community-based health and social services for prevention, intervention, and treatment. Yet, in spite of the extraordinary progress, many hard-to-reach and hidden populations remain underserved, at risk, and in need of care for substance abuse, infectious diseases, and other health and social problems.

Researchers at the National Development and Research Institutes (NDRI) in New York City have prepared this book to address some of the practical challenges and complexities of conducting research and delivering services to marginalized groups and populations. Their expertise reflects more than 15 years of knowledge and experience in working with people outside the mainstream, including drug users, the homeless, street prostitutes, runaway teenagers, and drug dealers. Nearly all the authors of these chapters have responded to the numerous health crises associated with drug injection, crack cocaine, other drug abuse, and the rapid spread of HIV and other infectious diseases. They have worked in diverse environments to develop, implement, evaluate, and deliver a range of interventions and services. Their new, practical guide will interest readers from varied backgrounds and disciplines, who will find it helpful for planning, implementing, and conducting large public health

This foreword represents the views of its authors (Richard H. Needle, Ph.D., M.P.H., and Elizabeth Y. Lambert, M.Sc.) and not those of the National Institute on Drug Abuse at the National Institutes of Health.

research and service projects with marginalized populations, especially under trying and difficult circumstances. The chapters address a range of topics that will interest readers of multiple disciplines and backgrounds. Through this new book, Dr. Tortu, Dr. Goldsamt, and Mr. Hamid have succeeded in their aim of providing the reader with timely and practical information on research and service delivery with hard-to-reach and hidden populations.

Richard H. Needle, Ph.D., M.P.H.
National Institute on Drug Abuse

Elizabeth Y. Lambert, M.Sc.
National Institute on Drug Abuse

# PREFACE

This book addresses two recent trends. First, primarily because of the advent of Medicaid managed care, there is a need to reach marginalized and underserved populations. The fact that health care providers and social service organizations must make an effort to find hard-to-reach or "hidden" populations, many of whom need services, has had a major impact on these organizations. Hidden patients are often engaged in illegal or stigmatized behaviors, such as drug use or street prostitution, and they are rightfully wary of traditional medical and social service settings. Recent changes in welfare regulations have also created a need to access other difficult-to-find populations, such as the homeless, in order to provide them with training and education that can lead to eventual employment.

The second trend is the increase in the size and complexity of funded grants in public health research and social service. It has led to a need for researchers who can also function as skilled managers, directing complex projects that are conducted in field settings and often combine health interventions or medical and social services with research and evaluation efforts. Thus, those who may have been well trained as scientists or clinical practitioners must learn a new set of skills: training and directing a large staff with a wide range of abilities and skills, addressing different ethical issues, and setting up cooperative links with other projects or agencies. Often, they may need to find and maintain contact with populations that have compelling reasons to remain hidden. Rarely does graduate or professional training take on such topics as how to train interviewers, supervise employees, or conduct outreach to find and maintain contact with hard-to-reach populations. We have developed this book to answer this need.

This book has been written by a group of experts in research and service delivery who have been working primarily in field settings with hard-to-reach or hidden populations. The knowledge this book provides reflects wisdom earned through experience. Over the past 15 years, the authors have worked with drug users, the homeless, street prostitutes, runaway teenagers, and drug dealers, and they have conducted research or delivered services in such locations as inner-city storefronts, streetside mobile medical vans, single room occupancy hotels, prisons, and crack houses. Each chapter author either directs or serves as key staff on one or more large projects and has written about his or her area of expertise.

This book is meant to be a practical guide. Its step-by-step format offers clear guidelines to the reader. Each step of the process involved in setting up projects and finding hidden populations is described in a separate chapter. The reader can use the entire volume for an overall understanding of the process or focus on a single chapter or group of chapters reflecting specific areas of interest. Case examples throughout the book are drawn from a wide variety of projects to illustrate the diversity of the topics covered. Our goal is to provide a firsthand look at the practical issues involved in running large projects in difficult settings so that readers will not have to "reinvent the wheel" to work with hard-to-find populations in difficult environments outside the mainstream.

We have tried to make sure that this book's language is as jargon-free as possible. Although we have not targeted it solely to the academic community, we recommend it as a supplementary text in research methods courses or as suggested reading for those engaged in clinical practica. We have written it to be accessible to readers of multiple disciplines and at various levels within organizational hierarchies. It may also interest those who are engaged in or planning careers in "applied research." At the beginning of a project, the book can serve as a set of guidelines for discussion and planning. During a project, the book can facilitate discussions aimed at improving how projects are run or assessing staff and community dynamics that may be influencing the project.

Chapter 1, written by Bruce Stepherson, invites the reader to learn about the outreach process to find hidden and stigmatized populations. Using his experiences in directing urban, street-based outreach on the streets of New York City, he describes the outreach process and discusses how to enter communities to conduct outreach. He gives attention to the different considerations that should be addressed in conducting outreach in both urban and rural field conditions. In addition, the chapter describes the qualities that make a good outreach worker and offers tips for successful outreach. Finally, the chapter discusses the major external challenges to outreach work, such as economic and political conditions, as well as community resistance, and offers some ways to meet these challenges.

Chapter 2, written by Gregory Falkin and Shiela Strauss, focuses on the skills necessary for conducting both clinical and research interviews. In addition to basic interviewing skills, the chapter covers selection of interviewers, interviewer training, and working in difficult settings such as prisons or public locations. Drs. Falkin and Strauss draw on their experience in carrying out street-based and prison-based research studies and provide useful insights into keeping interviewees engaged during the interview process.

Chapter 3 focuses on following and tracking hard-to-reach populations. This chapter is written by Kristine Ziek, Nelson Tiburcio, and Nadina Correa. Ms. Ziek coordinates follow-up tracking for a number of projects that work with injection drug users. Mr. Tiburcio and Ms. Correa are responsible for carrying out the tracking protocols on these projects. The authors share strategies for locating and maintaining contact with clients who may be homeless, in and out of prison, and actively using drugs. Their techniques, developed over years of working with these populations, can be adapted for any project that seeks to follow hard-to-reach clients.

Chapter 4, written by Stephanie Tortu, Thomas Hamilton, and Rahul Hamid, introduces the reader to the tasks involved in directing projects and managing the people who deliver services or conduct research in field-based settings. In this chapter, Dr. Tortu draws on her experience in directing complex research projects. Mr. Hamilton has had extensive experience in managing service delivery efforts targeted at drug users in New York City. For many years, Mr. Hamid has worked in a research setting overseeing interviewing procedures. The emphasis in this chapter is on providing practical management solutions to issues that may arise in managing projects of this type.

Chapter 5, a case study by Michael Clatts, Rees Davis, Marie Bresnahan, and Helene Lauffer describes the process by which several New York City agencies collaborated to improve services to homeless youth. This chapter describes (1) how this research and service team assessed and solved problems by using input from several perspectives, (2) the methods used to encourage cross-agency cooperation, and (3) how technology was used to meet the challenges of working in communities with scarce resources. The authors detail the entire five-year process—from the early organizational phase to the implementation of a computer network. Improvements that were made draw on the expertise of program administrators, frontline outreach workers and homeless youths themselves. The enhancements to the service provision system that were begun in the early 1990s as a result of this project continue to assist agencies today in meeting the complicated needs of this population in New York City.

In Chapter 6, Beatrice Krauss discusses the importance of being sensitive to the needs of the community in conducting research or providing services. She gives specific methods for sounding out the community and involving it in the planning and implementation of projects. Drawing from her experiences on the Lower East Side of Manhattan, she notes the unique and often untapped skills that social scientists can offer to community-based organizations and also describes what social scientists and service providers can learn from their clients. The reader will find several of her own proven strategies for playing fair and making the organization "of the community," not simply "in the community."

Chapter 7 reviews ethical considerations for field-based projects. This chapter, written by Sherry Deren and John Baumann, provides a background on ethical issues in research and service and illustrates how these issues apply to both traditional and nontraditional settings. Dr. Deren has addressed these issues through her numerous field-based research projects and her participation on NDRI's institutional review board. Dr. Baumann has addressed these issues for NDRI as a whole in his roles as grant liaison officer (working with all funding agencies), as deputy executive director of NDRI, and as a member of the institutional review board. This chapter describes regulations that ensure the ethical treatment of participants in research and service projects.

Chapter 8, written by Lloyd Goldsamt, describes the integration of service provision and research in a single setting. Dr. Goldsamt, an NDRI researcher and a licensed clinical psychologist, shares reasons and strategies for making this integration possible. The chapter reviews obstacles to integrating these activities from both research and service perspectives and suggests concrete solutions for overcoming these obstacles.

We hope that you find the information and ideas in this volume helpful in your work. We are confident that by sharing our expertise and provoking you to think about the challenges involved in working with hard-to-reach populations you will improve the quality of your research and enhance the delivery of services to those in need of them.

Stephanie Tortu, Lloyd Goldsamt, and Rahul Hamid

# ACKNOWLEDGMENTS

For more than a decade, our field staff has recruited, interviewed, and provided medical and social services to our project participants in a dignified and respectful manner. We appreciate the talents of the outreach workers, interviewers, counselors, social workers, nurses, and other staff who worked so hard to implement the projects described in this book. We also thank our NDRI colleague, Sam Friedman, for his careful reading and incisive comments on early drafts of the chapters. Lee Wengraf and Sherelle Bonaparte, also of NDRI, provided helpful clerical assistance, and Terry Ruefli, executive director of New York Harm Reduction Educators, graciously permitted us to use his photographs of New York–based street scenes.

We are mindful of the fact that the work described here was done in the midst of great human suffering. For the most part, our projects were conducted at the intersection of two major epidemics of our time, drug misuse and AIDS. The suffering associated with these epidemics has been disproportionately shouldered by the hidden and stigmatized populations we have studied. We hope our work, in some small way, has eased their burdens and moved us closer to a world that recognizes and honors compassion for those affected by these problems.

# ABOUT THE CONTRIBUTORS

**John R. Baumann,** Ph.D., is the former deputy executive director of the National Development and Research Institutes, Inc. (NDRI). Dr. Baumann received his doctorate in Sociology from the Graduate Center of the City University of New York in 2000. He is now the director of the Office of Sponsored Programs and Research Support at the University of Missouri at Kansas City.

**Marie Bresnahan,** M.P.H., worked at NDRI as the intervention coordinator for the Youth At Risk Project. Her experience with HIV/AIDS, substance abuse, and youth issues came from her work at Covenant House/Under 21, a shelter for homeless and runaway youth. Ms. Bresnahan is currently director of programs at the American Liver Foundation.

**Michael C. Clatts,** Ph.D., is a medical anthropologist whose principal area of interest is in community epidemiology and the development of community-based public health programs. Dr. Clatts was one of the first social scientists involved in HIV research, beginning with the first NIH-led study of AIDS in 1981. Since that time, he has conducted several studies that combined ethnographic and epidemiological research methods to examine HIV risk among several at-risk populations in New York City, including gay men, gay women, high-risk youth, and intravenous drug users. Currently, Dr. Clatts is director of the Institute for Research on Youth At Risk at NDRI and associate professor of Public Health at Columbia University.

**Nadina Correa** is a recruiter/interviewer for the ARIBBA 2 Project. Born and raised in East Harlem, Ms. Correa has been working in AIDS research since 1992. She has been an outreach worker on several different studies. Her job has included recruiting high-risk respondents to participate in research projects, distributing AIDS prevention materials in the East Harlem community, and running focus groups. In 1998, Ms. Correa traveled to San Juan, Puerto Rico, to assist in planning for a collaborative study between New York and Puerto Rico.

**W. Rees Davis,** Ph.D., is currently the project director of two research studies in New York City, one involving users and distributors of "hard" drugs in Central Harlem and the other focusing on HIV prevention on the Lower East Side. In over 11 years at NDRI, Dr. Davis has investigated youth and adult populations at risk for HIV and other sexually transmitted diseases, and for drug abuse. He has also developed new sampling methods for "hidden" populations.

**Sherry Deren,** Ph.D., is director of the Center for Drug Use and HIV Research and the Institute for AIDS Research at NDRI. Dr. Deren has been principal investigator on several NIDA- and CDC-funded projects related to drug abuse and HIV/AIDS prevention, and is currently principal investigator of a dual-site study of HIV risk behavior determinants for Puerto Rican drug users in New York and Puerto Rico. Before coming to NDRI in 1988, Dr. Deren was chief of evaluation for the New York State Division of Substance Abuse Services, where she was responsible for the evaluation of a wide range of drug treatment and prevention programs.

**Gregory P. Falkin** is a principal investigator at NDRI, where he has specialized in research on substance users, treatments for addictive behaviors, and HIV/AIDS. He has been the principal investigator for several National Institute on Drug Abuse and National Institute of Justice grants. Two of his current NIDA-funded projects are large-scale studies of treatment programs in New York City and Portland, Oregon. These studies examine issues found among women mandated to treatment, including HIV risk behaviors, domestic violence, criminal involvement, and drug use. Dr. Falkin also co-directs a NIDA-funded training program for 16 predoctoral and postdoctoral fellows specializing in behavioral-sciences research on drug abuse.

**Lloyd A. Goldsamt,** Ph.D., is a New York State–licensed clinical psychologist. He conducts HIV prevention research with inner-city families and injection drug users, research on drug use and violence in schools, and research on the impact of substance abuse training curricula. Dr. Goldsamt also maintains a private psychotherapy practice.

Based in New York City, **Rahul Hamid** has participated in projects on HIV and drug use since 1990. He has enjoyed being involved in all aspects of conducting field-based studies, from research design to project implementation. Mr. Hamid currently works at NDRI as senior research associate on a community-based research project and is also a graduate student at New York University.

As deputy program director of NDRI's Center for AIDS Outreach and Prevention, **Tom Hamilton**'s work takes him to the streets of high-risk drug-using neighborhoods in New York City. He oversees the activities of several teams of outreach workers who deliver risk reduction education and provide other services to drug users in field-based settings. A harm reduction practitioner and recovering person, Mr. Hamilton has worked in this field for over 14 years.

**Beatrice Krauss,** Ph.D., is deputy director of the Institute for AIDS Research and the Center for Drug Use and HIV Research at NDRI. Her recent work has focused on prevention in HIV-affected communities and on family adjustment to the HIV epidemic. In 1998, she received the Kurt Lewin Award for her social contribution in the area of HIV/AIDS from the Division of Social Issues of the New York State Psychological Association. In 1999, her highly regarded NIMH-funded program, Parent/Pre-adolescent Training for HIV Prevention (PATH), began replication in Mexico City under World AIDS Foundation funding; in 2000, the University of Miami received an award from NIMH to test an enhanced replication of PATH among Cuban immigrant families.

**Helene Lauffer** has had close to twenty years of professional experience in government and not-for-profit management, including past experience at the Twentieth Century Fund, the New York City Mayor's Office of Operations, and the New York City Department of Correction. For more than ten years, she ran a division of Victim Services, which supported direct-service programs for runaway teenagers, immigrants, the homeless, people with AIDS, and battered women. During that period, she collaborated with Michael Clatts on a study of the effectiveness of outreach on the high-risk behavior of homeless youth. For the past two years, Ms. Lauffer has been working as a consultant to not-for-profits, including the New York Immigration Coalition, the International Institute of New Jersey, NYC 2012 (the committee bidding to bring the Olympics to New York in 2012), the Ivy Athletic Trust, Citizens Advice Bureau, and the National Multicultural Institute.

**Bruce Stepherson,** M.P.H., is currently employed by NDRI, where he is director of the Center for AIDS Outreach and Prevention. He has also served as principal investigator of outreach intervention targeting HIV-infected individuals residing in single-room-occupancy hotels. A recovering heroin addict for 19 years, Mr. Stepherson has over 15 years' experience running community-based interventions and participating in research on issues affecting drug users. He is a founding organizer of New York Harm Reduction Educators, Inc./Bronx-Harlem Syringe Exchange and has served on community boards that address the needs of those affected by HIV, AIDS, and substance misuse. Mr. Stepherson has testified as an expert witness in court on drug users and their behaviors and has written about the effects on communities of substance use and misuse. He is currently pursuing a doctorate in public health at the Columbia University School of Public Health.

**Shiela Strauss,** Ph.D., is currently a principal investigator at NDRI on two projects. One involves a nationwide survey of drug treatment programs to identify the hepatitis C–related services they provide to their clients. The other, which examines the validity of self-report of HIV status, involves a secondary analysis of data collected among out-of-treatment drug users in 23 sites under the Cooperative Agreement for AIDS Community-Based Outreach/Intervention Research Program, funded by NIDA. Dr. Strauss has previously served as data analyst and project director on several other projects involving an evaluation of drug treatment programs for women offenders and an examination of the impact of drug treatment and social support in helping female offenders mandated to drug treatment to reduce their HIV/AIDS-related risks.

**Nelson Tiburcio** is currently a doctoral candidate in Criminal Justice at the John Jay College of Criminal Justice and the Graduate Center in

New York City, where he has specialized in Drugs and Deviance and Statistics. Since the late 1980s, he has had several roles on research and service projects at NDRI, including assistant project director, interviewer-trainer, and research interviewer. He currently serves as consultant field site reviewer to the Office of National Drug Control Policy for the American Correctional Association.

From 1988 to 2000, **Stephanie Tortu**, Ph.D., worked at NDRI in New York City, where she directed the evaluation of two large community-based HIV risk-reduction projects, and, as principal investigator, studied the impact of social context on HIV risk behaviors among female drug users. From 1996 to 2000, she served as president of the board of directors of New York Harm Reduction Educators, Inc., a community-based organization that administers a large syringe exchange program and also provides other health-related services to drug users. In 2000, she accepted a position as associate professor in the School of Public Health and Tropical Medicine at Tulane University in New Orleans. She teaches in the Department of Community Health Sciences and continues to conduct research on the association between social context and disease risk.

**Kristine Ziek** is currently a research associate at NDRI in New York City. After receiving a B.A. in Sociology at Queens College in 1991, she joined the staff at NDRI, where she coordinated and supervised follow-up activities for several large community-based research projects. In this role she devised numerous strategies for tracking and locating hard-to-reach populations.

# 1

# STREET-BASED OUTREACH . . . TAKING IT TO THE PEOPLE

## BRUCE M. STEPHERSON, M.P.H.

In the mid-1980s, HIV infection was increasing rapidly among the country's injection drug users, their sexual partners, and their children. In cities with a sizable number of injection drug users, public health workers recognized a state of emergency. The sharing of injection equipment was common among drug injectors because possession of syringes without a prescription was and continues to be illegal in most states in the United States. As a consequence, injectors were at a high risk for blood-borne HIV infection. Educational efforts were needed to inform injection drug users about the rapidly spreading virus, its modes of transmission, and available methods of protection. Techniques for cleaning injection equipment with chlorine bleach were available, and public health workers, often in the face of political opposition, wanted to get the word out as soon as possible to those at risk.

However, many long-time injection drug users have few connections to established mainstream health and service institutions. Often put off by the disapproving attitudes of health care workers and the fear of arrest, they ignore health concerns until a crisis occurs, then appear in hospital emergency rooms. How could this population be reached with AIDS education and intervention efforts? A major media blitz was impossible. Television and radio stations would not air public service announcements to teach safer injection techniques or urge the use of condoms. In addition, teaching such skills as bleaching needles and using condoms benefits from demonstration and face-to-face interaction, with an opportunity to ask questions and practice the skills. Finally, many in the public health community believed that injection drug users, in comparison with gay men, for example, were less motivated to change their risk behaviors.

In response to the challenge of providing AIDS education and prevention services to injection drug users, the New Jersey Community AIDS Program set up the first AIDS-related outreach project in 1985. The goals of the intervention were to reduce drug users' risk of HIV infection by encouraging them to enter existing drug treatment services. The group quickly realized that the recruitment strategy should focus on actively reaching out to drug users where they congregate. A special type of health worker was necessary for this task—one equipped with knowledge and understanding of the local drug culture and an ability to gain access to settings where drug users could be found. The project hired former addicts as workers because they would be more likely than typical public health educators to know both where to find injection drug users and how to gain access to these settings. In addition, their unique status as former drug users made them credible sources of information and more readily accepted by drug users. Information about AIDS was to be taken directly to the streets and to shooting galleries—wherever drug users could be found. Outreach workers were trained to provide instructions about safer injection techniques in many of the settings where injection drug users buy and use drugs. Drug users were offered coupons redeemable for access to 21-day drug-free detoxification programs, because stopping injection was deemed the best way to prevent HIV infection.

This first response to the AIDS crisis led to other efforts, and the models of outreach to drug users begun early in the epidemic were to have a major impact on public health campaigns in the age of AIDS. After the New Jersey project was underway, other AIDS outreach projects were quickly initiated in cities that had sizable populations of injection drug users. Although the main objective of all projects was to reduce the risk of HIV infection, each project put its own unique local spin on the problem. For example:

- San Francisco, 1985. *Mid-City Consortium to Combat AIDS.* Its goals were to increase HIV awareness among drug users by using community health outreach workers (CHOWS) to introduce a "Bleach and Teach" educational campaign. CHOWS took to the streets to teach safer injection techniques and to urge each drug user to teach the techniques to others. This campaign has been credited with keeping the rate of HIV infection among injection drug users in San Francisco relatively low in contrast with New York City, where political resistance to bleach use prevented a similar widespread campaign early in the epidemic.
- Chicago, 1986. *Chicago AIDS Community Outreach Intervention Project.* Its goals were to understand, intervene in, and contain community outbreaks of heroin use and addiction. The model was based on a multimethod approach that combined street outreach with the basic principles of medical epidemiology and community ethnography.
- Baltimore, 1986. *Health Education and Research Organization's Street Outreach AIDS Prevention Project.* Its goals were to provide information on HIV and reduce levels of risky behaviors among injection drug users.
- New York, 1986. National Development and Research Institutes, Inc. *AIDS Outreach and Prevention Project.* The project educated injection drug users on the streets and in shooting galleries about risk-reduction practices and encouraged drug users to enter drug treatment. No efforts were made to distribute bleach because of political opposition.
- Brooklyn, 1986. *Association for Drug Abuse Prevention and Treatment* (ADAPT). This community-based organization was formed

to empower drug users and advocate on their behalf on issues, including AIDS, that affected injection users and their families.

During the implementation of these projects, the workers providing AIDS education and prevention, now called *outreach workers,* were often the only ones operating on the front lines of the epidemic among drug users in the inner cities. They were typically the sole point of contact between the hidden and stigmatized population of injection drug users and the institutions that could provide them with AIDS information and prevention services, access to drug treatment, and medical services for those already infected.

As the epidemic continued, various models of outreach were studied and evaluated within the context of various AIDS-related research projects. Additional project goals included collecting information about those at risk for AIDS and evaluating the efficacy of the various risk-reduction interventions being implemented. One example of an outreach-based research program was the National Institute on Drug Abuse's outreach-based AIDS research projects. Designed to provide and evaluate AIDS risk-reduction services, as well as collect information about drug use, sexual behavior, and HIV risk behaviors, the projects were conducted in urban locations such as New York City, Chicago, and San Francisco, as well as rural areas and small cities such as Collier County, Florida, and Flagstaff, Arizona, starting in 1988 and continuing into the 1990s. Some of the issues related to street-based outreach in the context of such projects are addressed more fully in the book edited by Barry Brown and George Beschner, listed in this chapter's key readings.

The projects targeted injection drug users, their sexual partners, and crack smokers who were not currently enrolled in drug treatment. In addition, the research design called for multiple contacts with the participants; thus, outreach workers developed and maintained ongoing relationships with participants. These projects reached thousands of drug users, many of whom entered drug treatment, got needed medical care, or received referrals to social services. Testing various models of outreach, demonstrating their utility, and documenting both positive and negative experiences were instrumental techniques in developing more sophisticated outreach-based projects. Another objective was to bring this approach to the attention of social scientists and public health officials.

Today, there are new reasons for expanding the use of the outreach process. The drive by federal, state, and city governments to control health care costs and utilization rates currently dominates policy discussions among service providers, consumer advocates, and politicians. The concept of managed care—which restructures health care provision mechanisms, and often restricts access—has made it more difficult for disadvantaged and hard-to-reach populations to receive necessary health care. At present, outreach concerned with preventing HIV infection among drug users has been standardized in many areas of the country, but public health officials are raising new concerns about outbreaks of other serious diseases, such as hepatitis B and hepatitis C, and the recurrence of tuberculosis. Community-based outreach models can reach the homeless, runaway youths, sex workers, and other marginalized groups.

## GOALS OF THE CHAPTER

Using my experiences in directing a large, urban, street-based outreach program in New York City, I offer in this chapter an overview of outreach work so that the reader can understand how to organize an outreach team and meet the challenges of conducting outreach. The chapter is not meant to be an exhaustive representation of every known model utilizing outreach workers, nor is it meant to address the many theoretical paradigms that underpin various outreach projects and intervention approaches.

Specifically, this chapter will address:

- How to enter communities and build trust
- The functions performed by outreach workers and the qualities that make a good outreach worker
- How urban and rural field conditions affect outreach work
- Tips for successful outreach

- The major challenges affecting outreach work and how to confront them

## OUTREACH: A BOTTOM-UP APPROACH

Street-based outreach is designed to bring information directly to people in the settings where they congregate and socialize. We do not wait for the people to come to us—we go to them. Experience has shown that populations such as the drug users with whom I work are receptive to receiving information and direct services in this way. My street-based outreach staff in New York City informs, educates, and provides materials to active drug users.

We also teach them safer techniques to clean their injection equipment and work with them to get the services they need. This population often has difficulty getting into drug treatment, receiving public entitlements, and obtaining medical services. Other

*An outreach worker providing streetside health information in New York City.*

outreach teams in New York City visit areas frequented by street-based commercial sex workers and the homeless. Their services include diagnosis and treatment for sexually transmitted diseases and psychiatric assessments. Many members of the populations targeted for outreach will not or cannot access necessary medical and social services for fear of being identified to law enforcement agencies, the immigration service, or public health departments by medical and social service agencies that may have reporting requirements. Street-based outreach provides services while eliminating this risk.

One effective educational model that has been adapted for outreach was designed by Paulo Freire, a Brazilian educator. He advocates a bottom-up approach that recognizes the experiential knowledge and basic dignity of those being targeted. This model seeks to enlist, train, and develop leaders from within the targeted subgroups who can speak for and represent the goals and needs of the community. Bottom-up models arose in opposition to dominant mainstream models that are hierarchical and reinforce the power and authority of public health experts and research scientists.

Public policy, which follows the more conventional top-down approach, can have a drastic impact on the lives of drug users and other marginal populations. In one of my New York City outreach projects designed to bring drug users to medical, social, and drug treatment services, my outreach workers reported that some injectors were very anxious about the proposed changes to New York State laws concerning welfare and disability entitlements. Several users were worried that benefits would be cut off because, under the new rules, "addiction" to a substance disqualified them from receiving disability entitlements. During the course of conversations with the injectors, we learned that drug users believed that if they deliberately shared injection equipment with an HIV-infected user in order to become infected, they could retain their benefits. HIV infection would entitle them to continued assistance because their disability would not be due to active drug use but to the acceptable entitlement condition of having a disease. When I learned of this, I immediately instructed my staff to inform drug users that this was not an appropriate solution to the problem and was, in fact, a dangerous risk to their health. I also made a verbal report to the state drug agencies. Anecdotal reports, such as this one, can inform interventions and guide public policy debates. Outreach, with its bottom-up approach, can serve as a crucial link between people at the lowest levels of society and those who make policy decisions.

## WHO ARE THE HIDDEN POPULATIONS?

In many instances, groups that are hidden or hard to reach by traditional service providers are engaged in illegal or stigmatized behavior. Drug users, sex workers, and illegal immigrants are some examples. As noted previously, many cannot or will not access services in traditional ways for fear of "being found out" and reported to police or other authorities. Addicted pregnant women often avoid prenatal care they need because they are concerned that their children will be taken from them at birth. Teens who have run away from home and taken to the streets of New York, Chicago, or Los Angeles are often homeless, in poor health, and victims of violence, but many prefer life on the streets to an abusive situation at home. Illegal immigrants arriving in the United States from countries with tuberculosis epidemics often live in crowded and close quarters that increase the risk of infection but will not visit hospitals when they experience symptoms because they do not want to be reported to the Immigration and Naturalization Service (INS).

Such hard-to-reach groups do not receive needed public health information or medical and social services unless they are delivered directly to them on their home turf.

For example, in the early days of the AIDS epidemic, safe-sex information was delivered to gay men in bath houses and gay bars, and information about safer injection techniques was taken to drug users in shooting galleries. Reaching groups outside mainstream institutions has implications for addressing some of our nation's most pressing health-related concerns. By way of illustration, to control tuberculosis outbreaks, programs need to reach drug users, homeless people, and recent immigrants with active disease. To reduce morbidity and mortality caused by violence, programs need to engage delinquent youth, especially those involved in the drug trade. To reduce infant mortality, public health initiatives need to serve homeless and drug-using women who have disproportionately high rates of perinatal health problems.

## PLANNING OUTREACH STRATEGY

To be effective, outreach must be built on a thorough understanding of the community. Long before outreach workers enter a community, service providers or research teams must become as knowledgeable as possible about the environment in which they will be working and about the target population they will attempt to reach. Sometimes, project planners use the services of a trained ethnographer to create a detailed ethnographic profile of the community where the project will be located. Projects should pay particular attention to factors that inhibit or serve as barriers to effective service. Fixed outreach schedules guarantee the physical presence of staff in certain previously identified locales. In this way, members of the community and the targeted population get used to seeing staff in certain areas at particular times. The workers become known and accepted as "familiar" to the setting. In any of the interventions on which I have worked, this process of becoming known to the larger community has involved going to meetings of community boards or merchants' associations and attending community functions, health fairs, rallies, and political events. The information gained this way will guide the overall outreach strategy. In addition, a comprehensive plan must be able to react to changes in street conditions or to movements of targeted populations.

Another important issue to address in the planning stages is the selection of materials to be distributed to the target population. A project planner must decide whether literature or brochures are culturally appropriate, in consultation with representatives of the targeted population. It is also important to determine if the materials are written at the proper literacy level. Reading specialists can be of assistance in making this assessment. With populations that have literacy problems, instructions can also be provided via comic books. In New York City during the 1980s, Bleach Man was an effective comic book character who taught addicts better needle hygiene through pictures and simple phrases.

The final stage of planning concerns training outreach staff. They need a thorough grounding in the community where they will work, which is best acquired through spending time on the streets to become acquainted with the neighborhood. This training can be accomplished by teaming new workers with more experienced outreach staff.

In coordination with this informal orientation, outreach projects should provide their workers with a solid knowledge base and with skills appropriate to outreach goals. Workers in the AIDS epidemic must be familiar with the modes of transmission, methods of prevention, and available treatments. Staff who will be working with runaway youth must know which social service agencies meet the needs of teenagers on their own. Staff working with street-based commercial sex workers to reduce the risk of sexually transmitted diseases must be able to demonstrate the proper use of different methods of protection.

Perhaps the most important skill that an outreach worker must acquire is the ability to relate well and listen to the client. The ability to develop trust and mutual respect is also a significant factor in making successful referrals for contacts into drug or medical treatment. Therefore, the longer an outreach worker is involved with a client or population, the higher the potential for successful service or intervention outcomes.

On the street or in other outreach locations, interactions should begin with the use of a key phrase or "hook," which is an entry point into a more extensive conversation. The hook can be a smile, a mention of a local sporting or news event, a program newsletter, a casual joke, or a shared experience concerning children. The hook's purpose is to attract contacts and draw them into conversations that may lead to some level of engagement and mutual trust. Not all conversations have to be related to the program or intervention, but outreach workers must be able to engage people on a comfortable level that promotes their participation. Each person will respond differently to the approach, and experience will enhance the outreach worker's ability to successfully engage different participants from diverse backgrounds and experiences.

We learned a valuable lesson regarding trust and respect while conducting an intervention in New York City with HIV-infected drug-using residents of single room occupancy hotels (SROs), which house many HIV/AIDS-infected individuals who are otherwise homeless and receive public entitlements. Each resident pays the hotel manager rent that includes certain basic supplies (e.g., clean linens, toilet tissue, and soap). Outreach workers had a difficult time getting accepted in these locations because this particular population is wary and untrusting of strange officials, local authorities, and institutions that they feel are monitoring them or wanting something from them. As in other interventions, we wished to provide educational information and materials to assist these residents in protecting themselves from HIV infection due to sexual risk and/or drug use risk. But we were not having the success we anticipated, and many residents would not open their doors to allow even the briefest of conversations. One day, while talking with a resident, a worker learned that the communal toilets were frequently without toilet tissue, a situation that troubled many of the residents. Many of these residents are profoundly ill, and some cannot get to the communal bathrooms located on each floor or can do so only with great difficulty or with assistance. We can only imagine what it must mean to them, suffering from multiple symptoms, to get to the bathroom and find no toilet tissue available. An outreach worker brought this information back to a staff meeting. Program managers, based on suggestions made at the meeting, decided to provide toilet tissue to those residents requesting it. Overnight, word spread of free tissue, and outreach staff were then welcomed into most rooms. This single act of providing residents with their own individual rolls of tissue generated enormous good will that brought our project great dividends in terms of acceptance by the residents of this hotel. With this new acceptance, we were more often able to get an individual to think about entering a drug treatment facility without fear of losing his room. The SRO policy typically mandates the loss of a room if a resident is not present or leaves the room vacant for a specified period. Trust in the outreach workers' ability to arrange for such things is hard to gain, and this one act made providing such complex referrals possible.

In the minds of the hotel residents, this incident was an honest, equal exchange between intervention workers (who provided the toilet tissue) and themselves (who provided access and information). In turn, SRO residents perceived staff as legitimate in terms of their knowledge and skills, relative both to the concerns and needs of the population and to the objectives and goals of the intervention and research project. As demonstrated, street-based outreach approaches offer tremendous opportunities for workers to advocate for and on behalf of the targeted population. The process of advocating for a homeless woman and successfully getting her into a shelter or temporary residence gives the outreach worker credibility not only with the woman but also with her social networks, which makes accessing and providing service to a larger number of people at risk easier and more realistic.

## INCENTIVES AND PARTICIPATION

Some research scientists use financial or other material incentives such as food coupons to recruit hard-to-find research subjects. These incentives are offered to compensate for time spent participating in the study. Public health interventionists may also offer financial incentives at times. In such cases, if the intervention is meant to convey health messages and facilitate access to services, the project has to assess what kind of incentive is appropriate. Remember that the nature of the relationship changes when cash or items of value, which can be sold and resold, are exchanged. Financial incentives may be particularly confounding to health-related interventions that seek to change knowledge, behaviors, and belief systems. In such instances, subjects may say what they think the staff wants to hear solely because they want the incentive promised them on completion of the interview, survey, or focus group. If financial incentives are used, the program must attempt to control for the ability of these rewards to skew sampling schemes, affect the client–outreach worker relationship, and affect the reliability and validity of the data collected.

In our own street-based interventions, we use material incentives that directly meet the needs of the population we target. In this way, the incentive is neither conveyed nor perceived as a reward or compensation for some level of effort or information received. It is instead seen as something that meets an observed need. For example, commercial sex workers want and need various types of condoms, dental dams, or needle hygiene kits, so we provide them as vehicles to engage the sex worker in conversations that provide health-related information and may ultimately lead to referrals for further services. This material provision furnishes the street outreach worker with time to initiate a conversation. The lure of receiving materials lengthens the contact and allows conversations that might otherwise not happen.

For programs with limited funds, many nonmonetary or low-cost incentives can be considered, depending on the program's purpose and expected outcomes. Clothing, a hot meal, a warm place to rest, a shower, and even an attentive listener can be powerful incentives that generate enormous good will and facilitate project objectives.

## HIRING STAFF

Good talking and listening skills are crucial to successful outreach. The ability to listen, observe, process, and communicate information accurately and effectively is essential. Attitude is also important. Outreach workers should not position themselves as experts whose sole purpose is to control the encounter, but as recorders and processors of information that relates to the expressed needs of the client. Accuracy—communicating without embellishment or personal distortion based on personal biases or prejudices—is critical. There must also be the ability to document and verbally report observations and insights to program supervisors and co-workers.

If I had to choose the one most important attribute for a successful outreach worker, it would be the personality and enthusiasm of the individual. If an outreach worker does not like talking to people, is not excited about the work, or perceives the work to be insignificant, this attitude gets conveyed directly to the client. This message tends to turn off clients and make them unresponsive to requests and participation in outreach activities. Workers who convey to contacts that they are not important and are simply a number or a means to an end are in trouble. Communities and target populations will quickly know it.

Outreach and project staff must also demonstrate cultural awareness, sensitivity, and social tolerance. In other words, respect the population being studied, served, or intervened with. Hiring individuals from the communities being served is often helpful. In many situations, service providers, research scientists, or interventionists are working in a cultural and social environment that differs from their own. For example, in one of my interventions where outreach workers must locate injection drug users, we hired individuals from communities in New York City where drug use is highly visible. This selection helps in the development of relationships based on trust and information sharing between outreach staff and their contacts. Additional qualities of a good outreach worker include a nonjudgmental approach toward targeted populations and the ability to function in multiple capacities and roles. For example, outreach workers may function as facilitators, information providers, and teachers who inform, educate, and train individuals and communities.

On the organizational level, the same holds true for projects, interventions, or agencies concerning their character and integrity (i.e., their organization's community track record). I have received and heard negative and emotional reports from community constituents about organizations or community-based agencies. One example that comes to mind is a community-based organization that is successful in receiving grants and conducting service-based research in communities of color. Members of the local community board expressed dissatisfaction toward institutions and organizations that seek community support (which is given) and then plunder the community for information and resources, only to later leave with nothing tangible left for the community to build on. In essence, the project took but gave little value back. Good service provision, research, and interventions must give something back, and it must be tangible and long-lasting. If the organization or agency has a bad track record, even the best individual workers on staff face a great challenge in successfully completing their objectives.

To find good candidates for outreach work, we solicit personal recommendations from other outreach staff both within and outside our agency. We also spread the word via the social networks of populations we intend to target. If, for example, we are interested in accessing homeless people or commercial sex workers, we might seek to hire out of the ranks of organizations that assist these groups. We might also contact our local coalition for the homeless or a community group that successfully intervenes with sex workers and ask the organization to recommend potential candidates. We would seek to identify candidates from volunteer organizations who have experience working with the targeted groups. We would speak with organizers and operators of soup kitchens and food pantries, as well as with workers in sexually transmitted disease clinics. We would advertise in ways to maximize our ability to recruit from these nontraditional hiring pools— on twelve-step recovery bulletin boards, in aftercare groups, and in local community newsletters.

Some outreach projects train, develop, and hire local peer educators, members of the targeted populations who are trusted and accepted by other members of that community. In our work, we have utilized grandmothers, bodega owners, hairdressers in local beauty shops, and women who congregate in local Laundromats. Each was identified and selected because of a particular ability to broker relationships with people or for an ability to engage and to provide accurate information or educational messages specific to the intervention. The value of peer educators comes from their position not only as outreach workers but also as members of the targeted group, which allows them to provide sometimes sensitive information on themselves and their peers that might otherwise remain unreported. In our experience, peer educators have been valuable in alerting us to the effects of police sweeps on the location of the drug scene and allowing us to continue our work in new locations. Peer educators in Laundromats and beauty salons have given us access to groups of women who do not self-identify as hard-core drug users and do not hang out on the streets but who may nonetheless be at risk for HIV infection and in need of other services.

## MANAGEMENT SUPPORT
## OF EFFECTIVE OUTREACH

Project managers must develop and implement a formal process to oversee project functioning and to facilitate an exchange of ideas, concerns, and insights. The process can be weekly staff meetings and/or individual supervision sessions. Keep in mind also the emotional toll paid by outreach workers who are continually exposed to the effects of violence, disease, and death. In addition to regular meetings, it may sometimes become important to have a forum in which hierarchical relationships are suspended and concerns and insights can be shared safely. This type of meeting is best accomplished with outside facilitators who are not associated with project management, such as social workers, grief counselors, or other types of therapists.

It is crucial for management to provide an environment in which all members of the staff can freely express their concerns. I was once involved in a research project that used outreach workers as subject recruiters and project interviewers. One worker revealed in a weekly staff meeting that she felt unsafe when entering a particular housing development. The project, up to that point, had no incidents or reports that would have caused us alarm. Her report catalyzed others to speak regarding the same concerns, and we learned that a drug gang was in control of the upper floors of this building (where drug dealers were selling drugs in several apartments). Once all the information was processed and evaluated, our team decided not to enter that building until we had developed a relationship with the drug dealers so that our work could continue safely.

This worker could have remained silent and ignored her feelings. But she felt unsafe and was troubled by the stares and body language of the dealers. This worker made a decision to formally state her concerns because she placed importance on her personal safety as well as that of her co-workers who also had to go into that building. In addition, she wanted the support of her co-workers to change how the outreach was being conducted. She hoped to sufficiently warn others to the potential dangers they could face if outreach was continued with single-person assignments. Had staff meetings been a place where this worker felt uncomfortable, this serious issue would never have been addressed.

## URBAN FIELD CONDITIONS

Outreach by its very nature requires adapting to diverse and sometimes difficult settings. Factors such as weather, security, police actions, and public policy, as well as the structural environment, must be considered in planning outreach work. In our work with drug users in urban settings, we always team outreach staff in pairs because of security concerns. Decisions such as these, which have costs associated with them, must be made after considering the context in which outreach is to take place. A two-person team is not necessary for going to a local community board, town meeting, or school program, but two-person teams are important for entering shooting galleries or crack houses, where the risk to staff from theft or attack is quite real.

Managers also need to be sensitive to weather conditions. If the outreach is outdoors and the weather is cold or rainy, planning should allow staff to take contacts into coffee shops or other sheltered places to talk. We have a policy of suspending outdoor activities during times of extreme heat or cold. Staff are provided with water bottles during the muggy and oppressive New York summers. It may also be necessary to provide staff with proper protective clothing. For example, our outreach staff wear heavy boots to protect themselves from stepping on needles and other dangerous objects that may be found in vacant lots where drug users congregate. Also, an antibacterial hand sanitizer is a necessity. By providing these materials, management sends a powerful positive message to staff engaged in work that can be dirty and dangerous. These measures help to ensure the health and safety of the staff.

Sometimes outreach programs enhance their efforts by opening storefront offices or satellite locations where more intensive work can be accomplished, such as rooms in local churches, housing developments, or schools. The purpose is to provide a secure, quiet environment to facilitate and enhance educational efforts or service delivery. Our offices in Central Harlem, the Bronx, Queens, and Bedford–Stuyvesant are places where staff can go to have private and extended conversations with contacts. These offices also offer access to a telephone to make health and social service referrals.

I remember one particular incident in which the storefront played an important role. The outreach we were doing at this time was designed to engage people on the street and to provide education about AIDS risk reduction in association with a local syringe exchange program. Staff were very familiar with certain program participants and the "regular" members of that particular street scene location. A woman approached one of our workers in a highly agitated, distressed state, crying uncontrollably. A female outreach worker recognized her as a resident of the community and a client enrolled in the local methadone maintenance treatment facility, located two blocks south of our field location. The worker engaged the woman and learned that she had just been sexually assaulted in a nearby park. All attempts to get this woman to go with us to the police or to the hospital failed, and we were having difficulty handling the situation, out in the street, with people walking by. The woman refused to allow us even to call one of the local rape crisis centers or hotlines. The staff decided to ask the woman if she would go with the female out-reach worker to our closest storefront office so that she could "get herself together" and so that we could figure out what to do in a secure and private environment, removed from the noise of the street. The woman agreed. At the storefront office, the staff began a process of engagement that sought to get the woman the med-ical, psychological, and legal assistance we thought she urgently needed. As this process unfolded, the woman proceeded to tell us her story, which I'll paraphrase as follows:

> I was on my way to the [methadone maintenance] program and I decided that I wanted to buy some coke [cocaine] to do after I got my meth [methadone]. So I went down to the hangout [the local park where drug dealers and drug users are known to congregate] to see if I saw Mr. X. After I copped [bought the drugs], I was walking back down a trail heading toward the program when suddenly I was grabbed from behind and dragged down a hill and mugged, robbed, and raped. The guy must have saw me cop and followed me to take my drugs and money. I guess he saw me stash the coke in my bra because as he held me down he ripped my blouse open, asking where the coke was. I didn't fight him because I was pregnant and scared for my life. When he was done I gathered myself up—in shock—and you saw me as I was heading toward the program.

The staff asked her why she did not yell or call the police. She told us that she knew no one in that park would help her. She said she feared going to the police because she did not want her hus-band to find out that she was using cocaine again. She felt that if her husband found out, he would become physically violent with her. She feared that she would have to tell the police the truth and that her husband would probably find out that she was in a well-known drug-buying location when this crime occurred. Further, the woman did not want to go to the medical staff at her methadone program because she feared having to admit that she was using illicit cocaine, which would carry certain program "punishments" such as an increased pickup schedule, more rigorous urine testing, or an unwanted dosage increase.

These are very complex dilemmas; my purpose for relating this story is to highlight the fact that we were fortunate to have a skilled staff with access to a storefront office who could assist this woman in dealing with such problems. Credibility is gained, incrementally, by offering sensitive and compassionate help in crisis situations. Outreach workers who target hidden and stigmatized populations often meet people facing enormously difficult circumstances. Outreach staff are called on routinely to provide aid and serve as counselors, referral specialists, and service providers. Staff members need to think about, plan for, and locate safe places where staff and outreach contacts can go when a situation cannot be handled on the streets or in congested public spaces. The story ended when the woman agreed to allow us to call a local rape-crisis center; our staff escorted her to a hospital outside her neighborhood, where the hospital's crisis intervention staff took her in and worked with her to address the rape event and her fears of its consequences.

## RURAL FIELD CONDITIONS

Like urban outreach conditions, rural settings also offer a variety of challenges. Weather, distance, and travel are important considerations in planning rural outreach interventions. Outreach staff may spend hours in public spaces and encounter only a few contacts. Access to target populations is more difficult because of geographic distance and lack of good public transportation systems. The target population tends to be decentralized in rural areas, with a lack of public spaces where people congregate. To cover greater distances, vehicles are a necessity. In some rural projects, I have seen cellular phones and pagers used to make contact with people.

In rural settings, outreach workers must be able to gain access to social networks of drug users who, because there is no recognizable street drug scene, often meet in private houses. As in urban settings, community constituents (i.e., those community members who can be recruited to assist staff in gaining entree to the population of interest) are tremendous assets. Because rural populations tend to congregate in buildings, homes, community centers, and bars, community "helpers" to assist in locating appropriate contacts are necessary. Whatever the population or behavior of interest, indigenous informants can be developed, given patience and discretion. Many projects, interventions, and research efforts have social implications and tangible benefits for the targeted population. Often this "good will" helps to enlist support from some individuals who can be recruited to help in project efforts. Once local informants are recruited and introductions are made to the target population, they can lead to others. And, as mentioned before, having a central location where people can safely gather facilitates the staff's ability to collect more comprehensive data or provide more complete services. In addition, the outreach staff may want to visit clubs, bars, fraternal groups, malls, or political events to improve their knowledge of the area and the targeted people.

Sometimes creativity is necessary to find solutions to the challenges of rural outreach. One rural syringe exchange program acquired large trucks that were converted to provide several small offices and medical examination rooms. The program used these vehicles as extensions of its outreach operations. In other rural programs, commercial vans and station wagons are fitted with curtains or small panels to afford some measure of privacy for confidential conversations. These options are expensive because they require gas, maintenance, tolls, and repairs; if desired, they must be researched thoroughly. Do the expense and labor necessary to operate a vehicle make sense, and will the expected results develop? In one of my projects, we bought a vehicle in which we performed medical procedures and transported groups of employees and program participants to our storefront locations. Unfortunately, we underestimated the expense involved in insuring a vehicle with commercial plates. Although insurance rates vary by region, the costs were so high in New York City that this particular program is now considering selling the vehicle because the expense far exceeds its value to the program. Nevertheless, in rural settings, it may be the only viable approach to provide outreach to certain groups and therefore must be carefully considered in the program design.

## OUTREACH—DO'S AND DON'TS

As in any profession, there are rules of conduct and an accepted mode of behavior in the workplace. These standards should be clearly communicated to the outreach staff. We have found that the following general rules of street-based outreach go a long way in preventing problems.

### Do's (Outreach professionalism encompasses these aspects of behavior.)

- Come prepared for work with all the necessary materials to properly perform your job functions (e.g., pen, paper, referral manuals, program materials and literature).
- At all times, carry appropriate work and personal identification to verify your purpose and presence, if necessary.
- Carry emergency telephone numbers, such as lawyers' and doctors' numbers.
- Dress neatly; be well groomed and personable.
- Wear appropriate clothing and shoes (for weather and social environment).
- Carry comprehensive service referral lists to be able to respond to requests not within the purview of your program or intervention.
- Remember to conduct your outreach in pairs and to remain in visual contact with your partner at all times.
- Become known in the community and among the targeted population.
- Be respectful of people and places.
- Avoid expressing your personal opinions on sensitive or controversial topics (e.g., religion or politics) that may have a negative effect in conversations with program participants.

- Conduct your outreach in a consistent, regular, and visible manner so that the target population becomes familiar with you.
- Seek to defuse incidents that have the potential to cause harm, when possible. Should that fail, walk away!
- Listen. Be discreet and sensitive to your surroundings (e.g., to the unspoken messages and nonverbal signals people convey).
- Provide realistic help in a consistent and reliable fashion.
- Engage in a process of consequential thinking: Ask yourself, If I do or say this, what are the potential outcomes? And what are my alternatives if a negative situation develops?
- Try to be credible, honest, and forthright, and always guard the confidentiality commitments made to participants on behalf of your project.
- Encourage your contacts to pass along your information and materials to others they may know.
- Remember to ask for help when a situation goes beyond your capability to handle it.

### Don'ts
- Do not put yourself or the staff in dangerous or risky situations.
- Do not become personally involved with co-workers or with your contacts (e.g., by using drugs or having sex).
- Do not wear clothing or personal accessories that may create "distance" between the worker and the person engaged (e.g., expensive clothing or jewelry, dark sunglasses, hats pulled down over the eyes).
- Do not argue or use loud, abusive, or profane language when communicating with street contacts or community residents.
- Do not engage in, or knowingly facilitate, illicit activities.
- Do not lend money or items of personal value to contacts.
- Do not carry valuables or large sums of money during outreach activities.
- Do not carry any weapons.
- Do not physically handle any person, and avoid any violent interactions.
- Do not make false promises or convey false hope to contacts.

- Do not let your personal biases or prejudices affect your ability to convey the information you are being paid to deliver.
- Do not become judgmental concerning an individual's behaviors or worldview.
- Do not give verbal messages that are culturally insensitive or inappropriate (including the literacy level of the written materials you distribute) to the targeted population.
- Do not get angry or make insulting remarks when contacts reject information or materials.
- Do not force your information or materials on anyone. No must mean no!
- Do not forget to communicate with team members and project supervisors regularly and consistently.

## CHALLENGES AFFECTING OUTREACH

Whatever the model of outreach employed, many factors can affect the success or failure of program goals. Conditions vary, depending on the setting of the outreach. I want to discuss several factors that can have a major impact on outreach work.

### Social Conditions

I work mostly with individuals and communities devastated by poverty, drug use, HIV/AIDS, and other chronic health conditions. Therefore, my staff must be conversant with the latest scientific information on HIV and be prepared to address related health and social concerns. The orientation of the staff cannot be too narrowly focused. Their perspective must be holistic in order to address the basic social and medical needs of the targeted population. Communities affected by HIV may also include people with untreated or drug-resistant tuberculosis, sexually transmitted diseases, hepatitis, and alcoholism.

If an intervention or program is situated within certain racial/ethnic or religious communities, it must be sensitive to the needs and values attached to these communities and recognize the intraethnic differences within them. I have found that it is beneficial to hire a staff that represents the community in which I plan to conduct the intervention. Such workers tend to speak in languages familiar to the community and are more likely to be sensitive to its idiosyncrasies.

Outreach programs must also recognize the significant impact that lack of education and financial resources within the community plays in the ability to mount an effective program or intervention. If the target population is hungry or in need of shelter, these problems must be addressed before heart disease or breast cancer. One of the strategies we employ to assist us in working on these issues with contacts is to establish meaningful linkage agreements with other social and medical service providers. Through linkage arrangements and coalition-building groups among like-missioned organizations, we can bridge service requests to agencies or local community-based organizations to handle particular concerns that our program does not directly address. In this book, Chapter 5 discusses in greater detail establishing linkages among several community organizations with similar goals.

## Political and Economic Conditions

Politically inspired social agendas, legislated on either the local, state, or national level, can also present challenges for community-based programs. At present, our nation is in an era of managed health care, which is having a significant impact on those receiving federal, state, and local entitlements. In this social environment, the challenge for staff is to help program participants overcome barriers in accessing the services they need. Old methods of assisting individuals who request access to substance abuse treatment services are further complicated by new political mandates. An example is the change in eligibility requirements for those requesting and those already receiving public assistance in New York State. People who are physically able and no longer defined as biomedically addicted to drugs must now participate in work experience programs (Workfare) as a condition of continued public entitlements. This change requires outreach workers to better assess an individual's drug dependency and to help clients devise creative methods to survive. As health care costs continue to escalate and our political leaders search for ways to control them, access to and control over who is entitled to services will continue to confound our interventions. The challenge for outreach workers and program managers, therefore, is to acquire the skills (client advocacy) and knowledge (entitlement systems, treatment modalities and entrance requirements, etc.) to effectively adapt to potential changes.

Additional political and social challenges are associated with:

- Changes in service-providing agencies (e.g., program mission or resources)
- Structural changes (e.g., changes in entitlement definitions and syringe laws)
- Physical changes (e.g., building demolition or highway construction projects)
- Changes that occur within funding agencies (e.g., budget cuts or revised funding priorities)

These changes usually result from shifts in leadership, political differences among those in positions of influence and authority, differences in philosophical approach, or differences in economic priorities or necessities. Some of these roadblocks can prove fatal to an agency's efforts. To survive them, an outreach project must be ready to adapt. This is why the groundwork done prior to the start of the project is so important. It makes agency staff aware of the social context within which a project takes place and, hopefully, ready to implement alternative solutions from a wide array of resources.

## Law Enforcement

Recently, there was a major police initiative launched by the mayor of New York City to remove drug users and sellers from the streets of certain local communities. This law enforcement initiative was targeted to specific communities with a high incidence of drug use and sales. The criteria police used matched the criteria with which we select our street-based outreach locations for finding drug users. Overnight, the police dramatically changed the environment in which we conduct street-based outreach interventions. Access to injection locations became more difficult, and known drug users and dealers would no longer stop and talk with intervention staff. Our street-based drug-using contacts (needle sellers, drug marketers, "touters," etc.) were reluctant to be seen taking our risk-reduction materials (condoms, needle and hygiene cleaning kits) because they feared the police would stop them and confiscate the materials. In essence, the police use the presence of these materials as an invitation to stop, search, and detain program contacts. The police act on the assumption that only active drug users ask for or take needle-cleaning materials. Our experience has been that many who are not drug users often ask for materials to assist a family member or friend. I recommend, when it is possible, trying to work with the community affairs officer of the local police precinct, while protecting clients' confidentiality, so that the project can operate with some level of cooperation with and noninterference by the police.

## Community Resistance

Whenever an agency plans to work among drug users, commercial sex workers, or other stigmatized populations, it experiences some level of community opposition or resistance. We have found that if staff can identify a common concern that affects a majority of the community's constituents, the project can develop a foundation from which to build individual and community support for our specific program objectives. In working among drug users, our approach in one community was to focus on the generic health concerns of this local community. Access to appropriate health care and the quality of that care were issues with an impact on every constituent within this community.

In an attempt to overcome some community resistance to our project, the staff attended local community board meetings and health committee meetings and identified the factors on which outreach staff and various community constituencies could agree. We offered our help in working with community representatives to address the concerns they identified as important. In this way, it was easier for us to ask for their support later on the less popular concerns that were important to us. These included enlisting their support in helping drug users change their behavior and reworking the community's perceptions and norms related to this problem. Through these meetings, the staff identified public safety and street crime as the dominant concerns of the larger community. Had the outreach staff initially gone in and made our case based only on the public health implications of injection drug use, I doubt that we would have been able to garner any community support. Broaching the subject was easier after we had a track record in the community. We framed our approach in terms and language that community constituents would recognize and accept. We spoke of "creating safe corridors" and "removing drug users from the streets." Although the intervention did not specifically have this mission, our outreach team demonstrated that we could help the larger community address these issues. The outreach workers can serve as a bridge between individual constituents and the larger community and hopefully help to diffuse and possibly prevent overt acts of crime. Because our work is street-based, outreach staff can assist in keeping those "safe spaces and corridors" for schoolchildren, the elderly, and other community members.

## CONCLUSION

Maintenance of morale, enthusiasm, and the motivations necessary to conduct high-quality outreach is an ongoing challenge. Outreach efforts that require continued interaction with populations such as drug users and the homeless are emotionally and psychologically difficult on staff. Outreach staff are regularly exposed to the worst of the social, physical, and environmental conditions that most other people seek to avoid. Outreach conducted over a long period can become repetitive and boring, and the staff may begin to suffer from varying levels of job-related stress and burnout. Successful outreach takes these factors into consideration. To address these problems, supervisors and co-workers must always be able to freely express what they feel and experience during the course of their outreach day. This can be accomplished by having "down" periods when staff are able to unwind and debrief. This process can be formal, sometimes facilitated by outside professionals, or informal. The important thing is that it takes place, with sufficient time given to the process. Do not make the mistake of assuming that a regular administrative meeting serves this function; it does not. Debriefing periods could include an hour-long group session each week to share experiences and feelings that relate to the nature of the work, biweekly stress management sessions that include meditation or acupuncture treatments, educational seminars, or skills-building training. No matter what method is used, there must be a respect for the dignity of the individual, an adherence to strict rules and processes, and respect for the confidentiality issues relevant to the information expressed and shared.

## SUGGESTED READINGS

Brown, B. S., & Beschner, G. M. (Eds.). (1993). *Handbook on risk of AIDS: Injection drug users and sexual partners.* Westport, CT: Greenwood Press.

Carney, F. J., Mattick, H. W., & Callaway, J. D. (1969). *Action on the streets: A handbook for inner-city youth work.* New York: Associated Press.

Feldman, H. W., Mandel, J., & Fields, A. (1985). *In the neighborhood: A strategy for delivering early intervention services to young drug users in their natural environments.* In A. S. Friedman & G. M. Beschner (Eds.), *Treatment services for adolescent substance abusers.* Rockville, MD: Services Research Branch, National Institute on Drug Abuse.

Hartnoll, R., Rhodes, T., Johnson, A., et al. (1989). *A review of HIV outreach intervention in the United States, United Kingdom and Netherlands.* Report to the Department of Health, London.

New York City Youth Board. (1960). *Reaching the fighting gang.* New York: New York City Youth Board.

Spergel, I. (1966). *Street gang work: Theory and practice.* Reading, MA: Addison-Wesley.

Wolfe, D. (Ed.). (1992). *ADAPT outreach manual: Reaching substance abusers.* New York: Association for Drug Abuse Prevention and Treatment.

# 2

## INTERVIEWING SKILLS: STRATEGIES FOR OBTAINING ACCURATE INFORMATION

### GREGORY FALKIN, PH.D., and SHIELA STRAUSS, PH.D.

Interviewing is both an art and a science. In this chapter, we focus mainly on the art of conducting interviews. Some important aspects of this art are knowing what questions to ask, how to develop rapport with interviewees, helping interviewees to recall and give honest answers, and how to ask questions about sensitive issues. For instance, suppose we want to know why people engage in sexual practices that put them at risk for contracting or spreading sexually transmitted diseases (STDs). To address this topic, we would have to ask a variety of questions. To keep it simple for the moment, men might be asked "How many women have you had sex with in the past year?" "How often did you use a condom when you had sexual intercourse?" and "How do you feel about using condoms?" Women might be asked similar questions, but the questions would have to be phrased differently because women do not "use condoms" in the same way men do. Of course, the interview needs to be conducted in a way to make the interviewee feel comfortable in answering these kinds of questions. But knowing how to get to the truth involves more than making the participant comfortable; first comes knowing how to get good information. Which questions should be asked? This is exactly where the art and science of interviewing come together.

The heart of interviewing is knowing how to get good information about the population served. Among the important things that need to be considered to get good information are what questions to ask, whom to interview, where to conduct the interviews, how to encourage people to participate, and consistency about the information requested. In the following pages, we focus in a very practical way on conducting interviews to get good information about populations with multiple needs.

First, we give an overview of what interviews are all about, and why we even do them, contrasting research and clinical interviews. The rest of the chapter discusses the art of conducting any type of interview by thinking about interviewing as a process. In "Getting Started," we discuss decisions made prior to interviewing, particularly why and how the interviews will be conducted. We then consider who will actually conduct the interviews. This issue is intriguing in a field whose practitioners are familiar with their clients and often stretched to their limits in the daily activities of managing caseloads and providing services. Once the basic line of questioning is planned and interviewers are on board, decisions need to be made about where to conduct the interviews. The interview should then be practiced and corrections made to improve it before the interviews are begun in earnest. Although many interviewers enter the process after these decisions have already been made, we wish to explain the often complicated rationales that lead up to these choices. Interviewers will then better understand their role and perhaps contribute to future interviewing decisions. The core section of the chapter discusses the actual process of conducting interviews, including building rapport, asking about sensitive topics, getting good information, keeping participants engaged, and recognizing participant styles and needs that may affect an interview. Because of the importance of obtaining good information, we also discuss quality assurance. The chapter concludes with a brief discussion about what happens after interviews are completed.

## GETTING STARTED

Interviews are conducted for a variety of reasons. The two types of interviews we focus on here are clinical and research interviews. Although the two often overlap, the content and structure of these two types of interviews differ in several important ways. Clinical interviews are mostly conducted for assessment purposes, and their primary goal is to gather enough good information to determine what services to provide to individuals. These services may include, but are certainly not limited to, hospital admission in psychiatric interviewing, providing public assistance based on the interview of a welfare case worker, providing appropriate and relevant information in the case of an outreach interview, and simply making an appropriate referral.

Research interviews, by contrast, are conducted to learn how programs could better serve their clients. These interviews are also conducted for other reasons, such as to evaluate the effectiveness of a program or intervention, to assess the needs of a population, to gain insight into the kinds of interventions that might be successful in preventing certain problems, to obtain information that can be used in a proposal to justify funding additional services, and to understand why people behave the way they do. In the main, research interviews are conducted to obtain accurate information that can answer questions about a population in general.

Researchers and practitioners also have different perspectives on what is "good" information. From a clinical perspective, information is useful (has practical value) if it helps to clarify who the individual is—what a person's needs and problems are—and provides insight into the kinds of services that will be appropriate for each person. Although there are various approaches to obtaining good information—ranging from casual conversations to asking questions from an agency's own psychosocial assessment to conducting a highly structured standard diagnostic interview—the evaluation of the client and the decision as to which services to provide invariably require intuition or a good sixth sense about people. Research interviews, however, often seek complete objectivity and elimination of interviewers' intuition. This objectivity is necessary because research methodology usually requires that the participants in a study are representative of the population as a whole and that questions are asked of each individual in a consistent manner.

Although we will discuss various aspects of conducting interviews, such as deciding whom and where to interview, training interviewers, and building rapport with participants, the underlying structure of the interview is the focus here. What questions should be asked in an interview? This section sets the stage for interviewing by discussing several issues that need to be considered in a planning stage. The basic idea is that, before interviews are begun, the process must be thought through in a careful and deliberate way. There is a high price to pay down the road for prematurely launching into interviews without adequate preparation. This preparation means having a very clear understanding of the purpose of the interviews (what we call a "clear picture of the end result"), who will be interviewed, and what kinds of questions will be asked. For interviewers who join an agency or a project after the interviews have already been developed or selected, an understanding of this process will facilitate a better understanding of the interview and its rationale.

The interviewing process begins with clarifying the main interview question(s). When interviews produce information that is not particularly useful, the problem can often be traced back to a lack of clarity as to the purpose of the interview. For this reason, it is imperative to spend some time thinking through exactly what is supposed to be gained by interviewing. For example, suppose a hospital is interested in creating a drug treatment program. The doctors and social workers already know that many of their patients use illegal drugs, including crack and heroin. They also believe that many of the drug users have serious psychological problems. What kind of drug treatment program should be created? To what extent will setting up a drug treatment program require psychiatric services? Interviews might be conducted with patients to answer these questions. If the end result is to produce a report for the hospital administration justifying the need for drug treatment and possibly psychiatric services, it is important to know what kind of information will be helpful to the administrators who will decide whether to approve a new program. When it is determined how the information will ultimately be used, specific interviews can be selected or developed to meet this purpose. If interviews are chosen prior to determining what they will be used for, it is unlikely that the interviewing process will provide the most useful information.

For another example, suppose a community group is interested in getting more information about people who inject drugs so that it can develop an intervention to reduce the spread of HIV. The questions that will be asked should be guided by knowing that the end result is to develop an intervention. This clear picture of the objective may be used throughout the development, implementation, and evaluation of the intervention. To develop the intervention, this group might conduct interviews with street addicts to learn more about injection practices. Where do addicts get needles? Under what circumstances do they share needles? Do they clean their needles? When the intervention is developed, it may begin by assessing this information for each participant. Evaluation of the intervention could involve asking these questions prior to the intervention and then again at a later time. The clear picture developed at the start of the interview process helps to provide a focus for many other aspects of the program.

Once the goal of the interview is clear, it is possible to decide the specific questions to ask. There are two basic interviewing styles or approaches. One involves asking open-ended questions as part of what is usually called a semistructured interview. The other approach involves asking close-ended questions during a structured interview. The decision as to which type of interview to conduct rests on knowing how the information will be used.

Interviews are intended to obtain information that can clarify our understanding of various phenomena from a qualitative or quantitative perspective or from a combination of both. Suppose we want to learn more about adult women who have been victims of abuse. We may want to know what types of physical and sexual abuse a group of women have encountered. We may want to know how often the women have been subjected to various kinds of abuse. How serious is the abuse? These kinds of concerns, which involve measuring types and frequencies of events, require quantification of information.

Then again, we may be interested in understanding how the women are affected by abuse or why they stay in abusive relationships. These kinds of concerns need to be considered from a qualitative perspective. It is possible to combine both qualitative and quantitative approaches, for example, by trying to understand how women who are abused more often or more severely are affected by abuse in comparison with women who are abused less. We can do this by first dividing a group of women into two categories—according to some cutoff point that distinguishes "high" and "low" abuse—which requires examining the data from a quantitative perspective. Then qualitative differences (having to do with the effects of abuse on women) can be compared and contrasted between the two groups.

## KNOWING WHAT QUESTIONS TO ASK

Although interviews that obtain information that will be quantified are always conducted in a structured way, qualitative interviews may be done in different ways. Either a questionnaire is used, or the interviewer asks questions spontaneously, in a free-flowing way throughout the interview. It is beyond the scope of this chapter to address questionnaire development in detail (we recommend the Bernard book in the Suggested Readings for a thorough treatment of this topic), but we have some practical suggestions for how to go about the process.

In general, don't waste time by reinventing the wheel. Even professional researchers embarking on a new area of research often try to track down existing questionnaires to see if they can use a questionnaire or interview that is "tried and tested." There are times when whatever questionnaires exist are not quite right for the purpose at hand, yet modifying the questions is sometimes easier and quicker than starting from scratch. Although this is not always practical, searching for existing questionnaires should almost always be the first step. Even though semistructured, qualitative interviews are often conducted in a free-flowing way, and the questions that are asked depend on the answers given to previous questions, we highly recommend an interview guide. The interview guide lists basic questions and topics to be covered and assures that interviews are complete and consistent. It is sometimes possible to obtain questionnaires for these kinds of interviews from researchers who have done work on the same topic or from the clinical literature.

There are a number of ways to find questionnaires. Clearinghouses are often helpful in this regard. Several federal agencies, such as the Center for Substance Abuse Treatment (CSAT), have funded the development of questionnaires and assessment instruments that can be used for research interviews. Their publications can be obtained either by contacting the agencies directly or through their clearinghouses. For instance, the National Criminal Justice Reference Service and the National Clearinghouse for Alcohol and Drug Information compile and disseminate government monographs that include questionnaires. One of the best "clearinghouses" to check is the Internet. Many research institutes now have Web pages, and surfing the net is a good way to find questionnaires on a given topic. Contacting researchers who have worked on the topic is also a good strategy. Check libraries or the Internet for publications on the topic, and call or write the researchers who indicate that their research was based on an interview of the sort that is being planned.

The thread that runs through this chapter is its emphasis on getting good information from interviews. The most important priority is that the interviews obtain information that is not biased in any way. It is imperative that the interview process begin without preconceived ideas as to what the answers should be. This point applies both in formulating questions ahead of time and in asking them during an interview. We have also mentioned the importance of being consistent to get good information from interviews: each interviewee should be asked the same questions, and if the questions are worded differently, word changes should not in any way influence the answers that might be given. Questions need to be clear and unambiguous. One strategy for getting good information is to cross-check or "validate" participant responses. In drug use surveys, this is often done by testing biological samples, usually urine specimens. Answers can be checked by asking the participant for the same information in more than one way or by asking another informant, such as a family member, to explain what he or she knows about the participant. Strategies for getting good information are discussed in more detail throughout the rest of the chapter.

## THE INTERVIEWERS

### Finding the Right People

Once the topic area has been clearly defined and the interview has been created or chosen, one or more people need to be selected to do the interviewing. A key element in getting good information is to make sure that the interviewer understands the interviewee. By "understanding," we mean sensitivity to the special needs and circumstances of the person being interviewed. For example, interviewees who are ex-offenders may suspect that answers given to questions about recent criminal involvement will be used against them. If the interviewer is aware of this concern, repeated assurances about the confidentiality of the interview responses can often result in more complete and honest answers. For other interviewees in high-risk populations, some questions in the interview may be emotionally charged. For example, women who were victims of child abuse may have a difficult time answering questions about domestic violence. The sensitive interviewer anticipates this problem and is alert to the interviewee's difficulty in responding to these questions.

Sometimes the person who created or chose the questionnaire is the one who will actually do the interviewing. Generally, this person is likely to understand the interviewees in the way we discussed. Sometimes, though, one or more interviewers need to be found to do the interviewing. Although these people can be sought by placing a help-wanted ad in a local newspaper, other strategies often work better. Notices of available opportunities for interviewing positions can be sent to schools in which there is a criminal justice department, a social work program, or any other relevant group of potential interviewers. In addition, those who have used drugs in the past and have been in a drug treatment program themselves are often familiar with many of the issues facing drug users and can elicit meaningful responses from drug users during an interview. Some interviews are best conducted by those of a particular gender, a particular race or ethnicity, or members of the potential interviewees' community. For example, to interview women on sensitive topics such as partner abuse, it is frequently best for another woman to conduct the interview.

## Training Interviewers

Initial training of interviewers, as well as retraining, no matter how experienced the interviewers are, is almost always necessary. This training involves learning how to ask the questions so that the most accurate and complete information is obtained. It may also involve instruction on how to record answers (e.g., as numerical codes, phrases, or complete sentences). If interviewers have little experience with the interviewing process, training may involve role playing, in which the person doing the training pretends to be the client as the interviewer practices asking the questions. When a more experienced interviewer has already been conducting the interviews, a new interviewer benefits by tagging along as an apprentice to see how interviewing is done. For the experienced interviewer, retraining is essential to prevent "interviewer drift," a phenomenon in which interviewers gradually begin to obtain information in an idiosyncratic way. When this occurs, two experienced interviewers may come up with disagreeing or contrary formulations of the same interview information. To prevent interviewer drift, have meetings in which interview data are reviewed, or have experienced interviewers conduct separate interviews with the same interviewee and discuss their interpretations or results.

The amount of time and effort spent on initial training of the interviewers depends on many factors. Interviewers experienced with both the type of interview being conducted and the group being interviewed may require very little training to conduct the interview, and those with minimal experience require more extensive training. How difficult is it to perform the interview? Is it very straightforward, with primarily yes or no answers, or does it require probing for detailed and focused responses? Are many of the questions on sensitive topics (e.g., domestic abuse, criminal or sexual behavior)? Are those being interviewed likely to fear reprisals if they respond to the interviewers' questions in a particular way (e.g., former or current offenders responding to questions about recent criminal activity)? In general, the more sensitive the questions for the group being interviewed and the less structured the interview responses, the greater the time needed to train interviewers who have limited experience with the topics being addressed and the manner in which the responses are given.

Training may also include how to complete interviews in difficult settings, especially interviews conducted in the field. For interviewers with limited experience in interviewing hard-to-reach populations, such field training is particularly important.

## DECIDING WHERE TO CONDUCT INTERVIEWS

Because field interviewing and outreach work are becoming increasingly common, another decision that needs to be made before starting to interview is exactly where the interviews will be conducted. In general, individuals with multiple service needs are interviewed either in natural settings, such as street corners, their homes, or fast food restaurants, or in institutional settings, such as schools, hospitals, prisons, or shelters. This differs from the traditional office setting in which most interviews are conducted. A hybrid of the two is the storefront, which is situated in the midst of natural settings to facilitate interviewing, but which provides a more traditional private, indoor location for interviews. Sometimes decisions about the population being interviewed dictate the setting where interviews must be conducted. For instance, interviews with hospital patients ordinarily have to be conducted in hospitals. Although interviews with prisoners are usually conducted in prisons, it is possible to interview them in the community after they have been released. Likewise, interviews with gang members might be conducted in the community or in correctional facilities that house youthful offenders.

Sometimes it is easier to gain access to the population by conducting interviews in institutions. But conducting interviews in institutions also has drawbacks, especially if the interviewer and the agency are not affiliated with the institution where the interview is being conducted. Permission must be obtained before interviews can be conducted, and it is sometimes difficult to find a quiet place, free of distractions, where interviews can be conducted with enough privacy to maintain confidentiality. Although interviewing in natural settings has obvious advantages, sometimes it is difficult and time-consuming to recruit participants. These various factors need to be considered in deciding where to conduct interviews, and sometimes practical considerations influence the eligibility criteria for who can be interviewed. For example, if offenders are to be interviewed and it is considered safer or more expedient to conduct the interviews in a jail, then only offenders who have been arrested will actually be interviewed.

## SEEKING INSTITUTIONAL
## SUPPORT FOR INTERVIEWS

Conducting interviews in institutional settings requires gaining the support of administrators and staff. Without their cooperation, it is not likely that the interviews will be successful. It is usually assumed that managers "gain support" from agency heads and department chiefs and that interviewers "build rapport" with study participants. However, once agencies or groups agree on an interview protocol, the relationships that interviewers establish with middle- and lower-level workers at an institution can make or break an interviewer's chances at securing contacts with and consent from potential interviewees.

This rule pertains both to institutional settings such as jails and hospitals and to community settings such as neighborhoods and storefronts, where local individuals act as informal gatekeepers. In either case, interviewers are the key individuals to gain this level of support and thus secure everyday access to potential participants. In fact, participants are usually the *last* group of individuals with whom interviewers have the chance to establish rapport. Interviewers typically have to "go to" and "go through" a range of individuals before gaining access to the people to be interviewed.

Although the conditions of such access differ by site, an interviewer can count on needing to get various kinds of permission from at least two or three different parties before actually making contact with the potential participant. However, each contact "toward" the potential participant can build support for the project. By negotiating the times and places to conduct interviews, by accommodating the rules of conduct at institutional sites and the terms of respect in individual homes, and by working with rather than against professional gatekeepers in institutions and local gatekeepers in community settings, the interviewer establishes and sustains the everyday viability of the project.

## INTERVIEWING IN THE FIELD

Interviews that are conducted in a clinic or hospital setting take place in offices or other familiar environments. Often, however, interviews in high-risk populations are conducted in neighborhoods where many of those to be interviewed actually live. Sometimes a storefront office is available for this purpose, but many interviews take place in the street, in parks, in people's homes, or in other less formal settings.

A special consideration for conducting field interviews is the organization of interview material. Three factors are important here: portability, confidentiality, and safety.

Although it sounds mundane, it is important for the interviewer to be able to carry and manage all of the necessary interview materials, especially for interviews conducted outside or in people's homes. Interviews that cover hundreds of pages are often impractical in these situations. A good rule of thumb in designing or adapting materials for field settings is to imagine conducting the interview on a park bench on a windy day. An equally practical consideration is the fact that interviewers may need to carry all materials to and from institutions, such as prisons or homeless shelters, that are unable to provide secure storage space for materials.

A second concern involves confidentiality of interview materials. Many interviews are conducted with the promise of confidentiality, and records are almost always stored in locked files or with all identifying information removed. Because field interviews are transported between the interview site and the project office, they are vulnerable to being lost or stolen. It can be desirable in some circumstances to identify participants with code numbers on these forms and to add identifying information at a later time.

The final and most important consideration is the physical safety of both the interviewer and the interviewee. Field settings often have the potential for danger, especially when interviews cover criminal behavior, including domestic violence and child abuse. If this danger is not addressed, conducting a good interview can be difficult, if not impossible. For the interview process to be effective, the interviewer and the interviewee must both be safe and feel safe. In general, conducting an interview in a public place (like a diner or a public library), as opposed to a home, addresses these safety concerns. When resources allow, conducting interviews in pairs rather than having a single interviewer in the field is a good safety strategy. This arrangement works best when the two interviewers have a good working relationship and a sensitivity to each other's needs in the field. It means that each interviewer can count on the other to be alert for any situation that may compromise their safety. Providing a cellular phone to each pair of interviewers increases both the reality and the perception of interviewers' safety in the field. Having them check in by phone with another project staff member or manager before and/or after an interview is also a good safety strategy.

As is true of most people performing an important and demanding task, interviewers of high-risk populations do best if they are given opportunities to express their concerns and voice their frustrations. Many of those interviewed have a whole host of difficult life experiences and wrenching stories to tell. It is not uncommon to find that a female drug user, for example, has often been homeless and the victim of domestic violence. It is hard for interviewers, hearing these difficult stories, not to react emotionally. They need an opportunity to express their reactions to the information provided by those interviewed.

In general, knowing that their issues are considered important to the project boosts the morale of interviewers. Periodic meetings should be arranged so that the interviewers can raise these issues and feel invested in the team effort to see the project through to a successful conclusion. Certainly, the interviewer is a key project player and is on the front lines in collecting information. Getting good information depends, in large part, on the efforts and dedication of the interviewer.

## Practicing the Interview

Especially if creating the interview or finding a good questionnaire to use has taken a long time, it is tempting to just begin the interviewing. As with most things, however, there is often a real payoff in doing things in a deliberate and unhurried way. Getting the best possible information often requires a patient and systematic approach that takes everything in due time.

Whether the interview has been specially created or comes from an existing questionnaire, some of the questions may not work. Perhaps some of the words in the questions are not clear to the interviewees. For example, if women who exchange sex for drugs or money are asked about their "clients" and they refer to them as "dates," their responses may not address the questions being asked.

In conducting an interview on drug use, knowledge of the street names of various drugs may be essential, both for asking appropriate questions and for understanding responses or narratives. Sometimes the tone in which the question is asked needs to be altered. Some questions with a set of possible responses may not work because the set of responses is too limited (e.g., many answers fall into an "other" category). When interviewees are asked to respond to questions in one or more sentences, the wording of the questions may not result in the type of information being sought and so may need to be changed. For example, an interviewer we know asked injection drug users where they injected, and most responded "in my arm." However, the interviewer was interested in the geographic location of injections (home, street, park, etc.). Needless to say, the question was reworded. Sometimes these open-ended questions should be changed to those that require choosing an answer from a number of possible options. Before the interview is actually used to gather the information, it is important to determine whether the responses of the interviewees are addressing what the questions are designed to answer. If not, changes need to be made in the interview so that answers are not ambiguous and address the relevant questions.

Information about whether the wording works is one of the important reasons to have a practice phase for the interviewing (called a "pilot" phase in research). Once the interview is practiced on a number of interviewees, it may also become clear that additional questions need to be asked to get complete information. Some questions may be unnecessary. Other questions may need to be substituted or substantially changed for those that do not work. Especially if the interview is long, it is important to ask only those questions for which a response will be useful; extra questions tire the interviewer and the interviewee. Because many of the populations described in this book do not have much staying power, interviews need to be kept as short as possible without sacrificing important information. It may also happen that interviews are conducted in a location that limits their length; a quiet room may be available, for example, for only an hour each day for the purpose of doing the interview.

Changes in the interview format should not be made after each interview is conducted; it is important to see if the same issues in the questions come up several times. Midway through the practice phase is the best time to make the necessary changes and to continue to practice the interview with the reworded or new set of questions. If more than one interviewer has been practicing the interview, this is also a good time for all of the interviewers to discuss how the interview is working and the changes that should be made. In some circumstances, the interview can be shared with selected members of the population to be interviewed; these "respondents" often make valuable wording, phrasing, or content suggestions For example, drug users may suggest specific drugs to cover or specific features of drug use that interviewers and project developers may be unaware of. At the end of the practice phase, final changes should be made to the interview after a careful review of what was learned.

A decision should be made at the outset in terms of how long and/or on how many clients the interview will be practiced. This decision will depend on the size of the project and the importance of getting it off the ground. Remember that the goal of interviewing is to gather objective and consistent information. This goal will be achieved only if everyone interviewed is asked the same set of questions, using the same words. It is therefore important to not change the interview once formal interviewing has begun. Too much objective information is lost if questions continue to be modified. However, regular (monthly, quarterly) interviewer team meetings to discuss the interview process and content may be helpful. At these meetings, questions may be modified in certain circumstances (e.g., when it becomes important to ask about a new drug of abuse or new medical conditions or treatments relevant to the interview topic).

## Conducting Interviews

Often individuals conducting interviews assume different roles at other times. Whether the interviewer is a clinician, service provider, administrator, or researcher by trade, it is important to communi-

cate and delineate the interviewer role when conducting interviews. This process is ongoing in varied settings where the formal
boundaries of the interviewer role and the formal process of the
interview itself must be created by those doing the interviewing.

The role of interviewer is not a common function in most institutions, where interviewing is typically subsumed within clinical
or custodial practice. When going into a residential facility to conduct interviews with women in drug treatment, for example, the
interviewer's purpose for entering the facility may not always be
immediately apparent to clients or staff. Clients may ask whether
the interviewer is "the new counselor," a Narcotics Anonymous
group leader, "one of the new clients from jail," "the acupunctur-
ist," or a probation officer coming to arrest a client. Similarly, staff
may assume the interviewer is a member of the auditing team
scheduled to visit their facility or a parent who must return during
those hours designated for family members to visit clients.

If clients or staff are already familiar with the interviewer in a
particular professional role but not as an interviewer, it will be
equally important to distinguish the everyday functions from the
interview role. Clinicians with frequent contact with clients must
indicate that they are conducting an interview, as opposed to a
counseling or treatment session. Sometimes they may have to
clarify that a portion of the time together is for interviewing (e.g.,
the first 20 minutes of a 45-minute meeting), with the remainder
of the time devoted to "business as usual."

The interviewer should make sure that the participant is well
situated before starting the interview. Regardless of the type of
interview, the beginning of the interview is an appropriate time to
orient the participant to the length, various "parts," and structure
of the interview session (e.g., breaks allowed, parts that will be
audiotaped or videotaped, and whether the interview will take
place over one or several sessions).

Building rapport with an interviewee is often a subtle process;
it represents the true "artistic" part of interviewing. There is no
universal method of establishing rapport, but there are general
principles that can help new or experienced interviewers in understanding this process.

## Introducing Research Interviews

Clarifications of the research role can take place at the very beginning of the research interview and can be integrated into the process of communicating the purpose of the study, the conditions of confidentiality, and the rights of participants in the study. It is most helpful to begin by describing the purpose of the study and the ways that the individual's participation will contribute to worthy goals, whether these include knowledge about a particular topic or population or improved services for needy individuals or groups. By explaining the practical implications of a study and answering any questions that an individual might have about "the research," an interviewer enables the study participant to participate as a human being rather than as a guinea pig.

Whether the study has developed a lengthy consent form that has gone through institutional review (see Chapter 7) or is utilizing a simpler type of agreement to participate, the process of securing consent should not be hurried. Going over the consent form line by line, the interviewer can explain the various protections to the participant's identity, such as the assignment of numerical codes in place of individuals' names and the use of pseudonyms in any reported findings. In addition, the interviewer can describe exactly how the confidentiality of information gathered in research interviews will be protected. Studies of individuals who may have participated in illegal activities (from serious crimes to recreational drug use) or who have had contact with the criminal justice system can seek a federal certificate of confidentiality, which protects research data from subpoena and provides study participants with an added incentive to answer questions openly and honestly. In all cases, study participants need to be informed that the research interviewer is obligated by law to report any instances of child abuse or neglect that the participant might mention. Licensed professionals, such as clinical psychologists and social workers, may also be required to break confidentiality in instances of expressed suicidal intentions or impending violence toward others.

Rapport is often referred to as having an "alliance" with the interviewee. Researchers and clinicians describe the alliance in terms of goals, tasks, and bonds. In interviews, rapport is facilitated when the interviewer and interviewee have a shared understanding of the goal (gathering useful information) and the task necessary to accomplish this goal (conducting a particular interview). When the interviewer and interviewee have a good bond (relationship), the interview is both easier and more likely to provide good information.

Perhaps the most important factor in establishing rapport with individual interviewees is showing respect for the person and her or his experience. Different individuals sense respect in different ways, and interviewers should be aware of participants' responses to body language, verbal language (including the use of street slang and profanity), and tone of voice. Being on time for scheduled interviews, providing safety and confidentiality, conveying genuine interest in the respondent, and validating (acknowledging verbally) the respondent's emotional experience are all forms of respect. "Giving something back" to the interviewee is also a sign of respect. In some situations, providing food, referrals, or monetary compensation can communicate respect. In other situations, providing a diagnosis, sharing information about the interview findings, or simply providing emotional support as sensitive topics are raised can be appropriate ways to communicate respect.

## Asking Questions about Sensitive Topics

As illustrated throughout this chapter, interviews and questionnaires often cover sensitive topics or contain questions that are difficult to ask. These topics and questions can usually be identified ahead of time, and potential problems can be easily prevented. Before the interview is conducted, questions can be worded in an objective, nonstigmatizing manner, using appropriate language that seeks to gain information rather than assign blame.

Of particular concern to the interviewer and/or the respondent might be questions about specific sexual acts, practices related to injection drug use, or the demeaning ways that an individual was treated as a child or as an adult. Such topics and questions can be introduced in the interview with a brief acknowledgment of the sensitive nature of the questions and a mention of the benefits of responding to the questions openly. An assurance of confidentiality is also appropriate before questions are asked that may be difficult to ask or answer.

With appropriate training, interviewers can be "desensitized" so that they can objectively ask questions about topics that they themselves consider sensitive. It is sometimes difficult to determine ahead of time which topics or questions interviewers will need to address in training. Only by identifying the perspectives and concerns of individual interviewers will training help the interviewers overcome embarrassment, fear of insulting respondents, or concerns about respondents' emotional reactions. To this end, it is essential for interviewers to role play sensitive interview sections. Interviewer discomfort during actual interviews will invariably lead participants to feel uncomfortable and to provide a poorer quality of information. Conversely, an interviewer who is comfortable with sensitive topics can put the participant at ease and thus obtain more accurate information in a more comfortable manner. Repeated practice (with the opportunity to clarify misinformation) is the only way we know to increase interviewer comfort in sensitive areas.

## Getting the Best Possible Information

In interviews, "getting the best possible information" means different things at different points in the interview. Although accurate information is crucial, the accuracy of information that a respondent gives may be difficult to gauge during the interview itself. Even the consistency of a participant's responses may be difficult for the interviewer to assess. Regardless of whether responses will be analyzed for their veracity or their meaning, there are several approaches to interviewing that can assist the interviewer in getting the best possible information. Perhaps not surprisingly, these techniques focus less on the quality of information and more on the conditions and quality of participation of the respondent.

## ESTABLISHING AND MAINTAINING
## A SAFE INTERVIEW SETTING

As we mentioned earlier, safety, whether emotional, physical, or even legal, must be established for the participant. Physical safety is paramount. When the interview setting is or becomes physically threatening to the participant or the interviewer, a different site must be found. A woman's apartment may seem to be a safe enough environment throughout the first half of the interview, until her boyfriend comes home and starts smoking crack in the next room. A street or park may seem safe until a police car cruises by. A public street may feel safe during the day but uncomfortable after dark.

In other situations, safety might have primarily emotional parameters. As people have become more aware of the effects of violence, interviewers are often expected to be able to provide counseling services and/or referrals for support services to respondents who become agitated or otherwise "emotional" during or after their interviews. Ideally, interviewers can prevent the emergence or escalation of emotional disturbances during interviews by making respondents aware of referral options and by interacting with the respondent in certain ways. As a respondent moves through a difficult question set, for example, the interviewer can provide verbal and nonverbal cues that convey an appreciation of the difficulty involved in responding to particular questions. Nodding silently, making eye contact or avoiding eye contact, and thanking respondents for their openness once they finish a difficult set of questions communicate this appreciation. Sometimes, after a respondent has answered a difficult set of questions, a reminder of available resources can help her emerge from an emotional moment.

Sometimes the interview settings themselves mitigate against any feeling of emotional or physical safety. This is certainly the case with jails and prisons. In these settings, a combined negative and positive approach can be helpful. Saying something like "Look, I know this is jail, where you don't reveal your business" can be validating for the respondent. Saying something like "This

**Doing Observations to Augment Interview Data**

It is often helpful to round out the information obtained from interviews by observing clients' activities in programs or in natural settings. As in clinical situations, two types of observations can be used in addition to interviews. The first type involves clinical observations a practitioner has already made and wants to document for use in a current project. For example, descriptions of trends or problems identified from previous clinical observations may be used to set up the problem that will be further investigated by conducting interviews. For researchers applying for funds to study or provide services to "underserved" populations, clinical observations used to describe the need for research or services can provide valuable information about populations and their needs and identify gaps in knowledge or available services.

Observation can also augment or contextualize findings from the interview data. These observations can take place in institutional settings, so-called naturalistic settings, or both. For a project focusing on services for homeless families living in shelters, observations could take place within the shelter itself and document various family members' experiences from admission to the shelter to their return to the community. An interviewer could also accompany family members whenever they go outside the shelter, for example, to get groceries, visit other family members, attend medical appointments, go to church, or spend time at the park. In these so-called naturalistic (i.e., noninstitutional) settings, the range and content of everyday life are illuminated.

Once consent has been obtained and the parameters of observation negotiated, interviewer-observers can document their observations of participants' current activities in fieldnotes. Fieldnotes are commonly used in ethnographic research projects. The first draft of these fieldnotes—ideally written the day of the observations—can be quite sketchy and scattered. Some researchers prefer to write fieldnotes chronologically; others write them according to particular themes or types of activities. A first draft of some fieldnotes might look like this:

—3 P.M., walked to train w/ R. "Good to get exercise." (Hurt back, carrying stuff after tx.) Bldgs. of people she knows in recovery, & their stories. Liquor store, 96th Street. No longer threatens.

However, once sketchy notes have been written (in the office or even on the bus or subway while heading back to the office), they must be expanded into readable, detailed fieldnotes as soon as possible, while the observer's memory is fresh. A final version of fieldnotes might then read like this, with the researcher writing in first person:

After we finished the interview at 3 P.M., I asked Rhoda if she'd walk to the subway station with me. She said she'd love the walk, and needs to exercise since hurting her back. (She insisted on carrying all her own boxes into her new apartment, once she left the residential treatment facility. "I was just so proud to have my own place.") Once outside, we walked past the apartment buildings of a few people she knows from recovery and calls or visits regularly. As we passed each place, she told me about the people, their particular stories, and their special personal qualities. At 96th Street, we walked past a liquor store. Rhoda looked in that direction and said, "In the past, that bothered me. But now I can walk past it without feeling threatened."

Fieldnotes can eventually be coded and analyzed by themes or other patterns, or sections of fieldnotes can be selected and presented as vignettes that illustrate the issues people face in everyday life. In either case, the documentation of such observations will generate additional dimensions to a project and can enhance the data collected in formal interviews.

information is important to help you get the services you need" may elicit information in this context.

In such places, slight physical modifications of the interview setting—such as moving just a few feet away beyond earshot of a corrections officer or other inmates or speaking in a lower voice—can make significant differences in a respondent's feeling of safety. In psychiatric settings, it is often advisable to allow the respondent to sit near the door, which often puts agitated interviewees more at ease. Respondents' needs for safety have to be interpreted in a broad context as well. If interviewers have developed a noticeable "rapport" with corrections officers on the unit or with doctors and nurses on a hospital unit, for example, even the most sincere assurances of confidentiality or allegiance to someone participating in the interview may be interpreted as meaningless.

## RESISTANCE, EAGERNESS TO PLEASE, AND ENGAGEMENT

In social work practice, resistance is typically understood in relation to the need for client compliance (e.g., with medication schedules, treatment plans, or clinic appointments). Any behaviors indicating that the client refuses or is ambivalent about participating have traditionally been viewed as evidence of resistance and in many cases as justifying punitive responses. Fortunately, in recent years this perspective on client participation has begun to change in favor of more supportive approaches to securing a client's full participation in treatment or other services.

A similar paradigm shift has occurred in research as well. However, unlike clinical practice, in which (eventual) health or economic benefits are seen as the "incentive" for participation in clinical or social services, the individual benefits of participating in research are sometimes ambiguous. As a result, researchers have attempted to offer various material incentives to potential participants, including small or large cash payments and gift certificates for necessary items like food or clothing. In years past, inmates participating in interviews in jails or prisons often received free cigarettes for their participation; however, public health aware-ness has reduced if not eliminated this practice. In some clinical settings, incentives such as carfare, meals, and even small sti-pends have become common practice as a way to increase client participation in services, and the provision of free treatment has often been an incentive to participate in psychiatric and other medical research.

Still, incentives do not always ensure individuals' eager or full participation in interviews. In custodial institutions such as drug treatment programs and correctional facilities, policies may restrict or even prohibit the distribution of incentives to partici-pants. Interviewers need to be prepared, then, to make the inter-view as comfortable as possible for the participant and to communicate the value of the individual's participation through-out the course of the interview; the goal can be to make partici-pating in the interview a reward in itself.

Resistance, as an expression of perceived power inequities within or beyond the interviewer–respondent interaction, needs to be understood, along with its nonidentical twin, eagerness to please. Because interviewers typically perceive resistance as a per-sonal insult, a personal rejection, a passive-aggressive gesture, or a signal that the participant is "asking for a fight," these behav-iors usually gain the most attention in an interview. As a result, interviewers are rarely attuned to interview participants who are all too eager to please, who "willingly" answer all questions with-out hesitation (i.e., without thought), and who give answers they think the interviewer "wants" or answers that may serve their per-ceived needs, such as being discharged from a hospital or being eligible for a research study. Interviewers must be keenly aware of this possibility with respondents who have been through similar interviews before, because these respondents may have learned to "speak the interviewer's language." As artifacts of perceived power inequities, resistance and eagerness to please can present the interviewer with opportunities to develop and test a range of interviewing skills that can be honed only over time, through a trial-and-error process that can be made less personally painful with the provision of skilled supervision.

In lengthy interviews, respondents may begin to feel tired or restless, in which case interviewers can cajole individuals to "hang in there," asking if they need to take a break, speed up, or slow down the interview. Sometimes a stopwatch approach helps give a flow to lengthy interviews with structured response options: "Five more minutes in this section, and then we'll move on to the last part."

It is important to always keep in mind the circumstances of the population being interviewed and the complex contexts of seemingly simple behaviors. Nodding off is a classic example. Drug treatment clients typically are sleep-deprived and held to demanding regimens in their programs; their occasional nodding off may not necessarily indicate that they are high. A woman who finds the domestic violence question set emotionally provoking may suddenly become tired and yawn dramatically during the interview.

When encountering these situations, interviewers can state their observations and keep moving through the interview to the extent possible. "I see you're yawning. We're almost done with this section." Sections of the interview can be broken up with moments of chatter or verbal expressions of suppressed emotions. At the end of a section of the interview, the interviewer can briefly converse informally with the participant, mention a humorous point about interviews or the environment, or otherwise momentarily "lift" the formality of the interview: "Wow. This interview goes on forever. Now I see why people don't like to answer all these questions!"

For participants who are not receiving material incentives for their participation and who are feeling frustrated with the interview topics or length, other "incentives" can be created by the interviewer: "Okay! Got through that section. Let's hurry up so you can head to lunch." Although there is nothing wrong with making the completion of the interview an incentive in itself, it does suggest that the interview may need to be shortened, reworded, or otherwise modified to be more user-friendly.

## ENCOURAGEMENT AND PROBING

Clearly, if there is too much missing information in a closed-ended, quantitative questionnaire, the available information may not be meaningful. Similarly, a participant's refusal to answer questions can limit the ability to interpret responses given in open-ended interviews. Rather than have interviewers take a threatening or punitive approach to this issue, respondents can be reminded at the beginning and at times during the interview that their full participation will ensure that their experiences and views are well represented.

The key is in figuring out what conditions are needed for individual respondents to feel comfortable with participating fully. The interviewer then needs to take the time to establish these conditions, if possible. Rather than prioritize the needs of the project, the interviewer should prioritize the needs of the individual participant and acknowledge early on the value of her or his participation.

It is best to avoid threatening the participant with the all too common reminder that the participant will not receive an incentive or will be punished in some way unless all the questions are answered. Interviewers need to have a very clear understanding of what constitutes getting enough answers for an interview to be useful. After making a range of unsuccessful attempts to encourage participants to respond to the questions, the interviewer needs to assess whether to continue the interview and may need to clarify whether the participant wants to complete the interview.

When a respondent does not answer a question, there may be several issues at hand. Interviewers need to be able to identify what the situation requires, and this can be accomplished by various types of probing. Rather than immediately interpret a respondent's silence as a refusal to answer, first the interviewer ought to ask if the respondent heard or understood the question. Questions can easily be repeated or clarified as necessary, and many interview forms can include specific wording for clarifications.

In open-ended interviewing, many probing techniques are available to interviewers. In general, there are two different directions in which to probe. The interviewer can restate the question with more specificity. For example, having been asked, "How did you get into mandated drug treatment?" the respondent may not be sure how to answer. The interviewer can then ask a more specific question that is vivid with detail: "I mean, when you were in jail, and you went to court, how did they decide to give you a program?"

In contrast, the interviewer can restate the question more generally, giving the respondent more room in which to answer: "Tell me how you got here." Such wide-open probes usually yield some kind of response, which can then be probed further for specificity, if needed. These two techniques can also be combined by counterposing one general and one detailed statement: "Tell me how you got here. You were in jail before." Many interview forms contain both general and specific suggestions for probing.

## MANAGING THE EMOTIONAL
## TENOR OF THE INTERVIEW

If the participant's behaviors make it impossible to complete the interview, if the participant is clearly uncomfortable, if the participant is unable to provide useful responses, or if the interviewer feels he or she is unable to continue the interview in a professional manner, the interview may need to be rescheduled. It is important to recognize when this point has been reached to avoid an escalation of frustration for the participant and for the interviewer. If the participant becomes too frustrated, any range of serious incidents could occur. If the interviewer becomes too frustrated, it is unlikely that the participant will want to meet again to complete an interview. Thus, the experiences and limits of both parties need to be monitored and respected during the course of the interview. In some cases, such as psychiatric assessments, completion of the interview may be essential to making a recommendation. In these cases, the respondent may need to be made aware, in a neutral fashion, that the interview will have to be completed later. (Note that in some settings the respondent's inability to complete the interview may in itself constitute a sufficient initial clinical assessment.)

Support can be conveyed in two main ways during an interview. First, the interviewer can help keep the interview flowing by acknowledging verbally or nonverbally the various emotional tones of the interview. Interviewers can articulate what they perceive to be suppressed emotions, and, if their perceptions are accurate, interviewers can momentarily lift tensions and keep the participant from getting stuck on one topic or feeling.

Even while articulating emotions, the interviewer maintains an objective tone: "These questions on domestic violence can make a person feel really depressed. I really appreciate that you're here, because we need to understand what you're going through." The goal is not to change the participant's feelings but to objectify any fragile emotional tone during the interaction and thus establish solid ground for the participant.

However, when listening to particularly harrowing accounts of domestic violence (for example), or when participants cry, become angry, or are trying not to cry or become angry during the interview, the interviewer needs to acknowledge the impact of the individual's experiences, without breaking the flow of the interview. Often interviewers can affirm the individual as a survivor: "You've been through a lot. . . . You're a real survivor." Interviewers should also ask participants how they are doing and assess whether they are able and willing to continue the interview past this point. Interviewers can tell participants that crying is okay, and offer a tissue, but they should generally avoid physical gestures of emotional support, such as hugs or back rubs.

If the interview is ended at this point, the interviewer has an ethical responsibility to secure support services for the agitated participant. This can mean referral to a 1-800 telephone crisis hotline; when possible, however, one-on-one support in person is always preferable. Those participants who are in a treatment program or other clinical setting can be escorted by the interviewer to a counselor at the facility. Interviewers working on projects that have a counselor on staff can summon the project counselor (by telephone or beeper) to the interview site to meet with the participant. Of course, all of these procedures should be in place prior to beginning the project, and interviewers should be aware of them before they do their first interview.

When interviews are conducted in jails and prisons, it is especially important to have a crisis support plan in place ahead of time, because bringing a counselor into the facility in an expeditious way can be particularly difficult. If a project plans to make a counselor available to distressed participants in correctional facilities, a permanent clearance should be sought for the counselor to facilitate unscheduled access to the institution. Last but not least, some form of support needs to be made available to interviewers who listen to disturbing accounts or assist participants who become emotionally distressed.

## ENDING THE INTERVIEW

Contrary to the common view that an interview is "closed" once all the questions have been answered, interviewers should begin closing the interview before all questions have been asked. Depending on various circumstances, an interviewer may begin to make a participant aware of the end of the interview 10, 15, or even 30 minutes ahead of the last set of questions. When an interviewee is anxious to finish, it can be helpful to build a sense of excitement in the five minutes before the interview is finished: "Congratulations. Only five minutes to go." Even though it may seem unprofessional to construct the end of an interview as a sort of horse race, in the real world of sitting through lengthy and anxiety-provoking interviews, this approach not only is practical but also reflects and even respects the participant's experience.

In some cases, interviews need to be closed—even momentarily—under sudden and immediate circumstances. This is certainly the case when a third party invades the interview setting (even by just entering the room) and makes confidentiality impossible. Whether a corrections officer steps within earshot of an interview with an inmate, a husband comes home from work and enters the apartment where the interview is being conducted, or the police bust the apartment next door, the interviewer needs to make a break between the interview and whatever follows. An interviewer may simply announce, "I'm stopping the interview here" and then decide (with the participant) what appropriate action to take. For each of the three examples, it may be possible to continue the interview after modifying the setting or moving to another setting.

However, in most cases, the interview can be closed "at the end." After all questions have been asked, it is appropriate to thank the participant, provide any promised incentive, collect the interview materials, and, in some circumstances, accompany the participant leaving the interview setting. Interviewers should make sure that the space used for the interview is put back in shape, free of discarded pieces of paper such as cassette tape wrappers and with tables and chairs in their original places. If possible, any contact persons should be thanked before the interviewer leaves the site.

Special consideration should be given when the interview has kept clients of treatment programs or other residents of institutions (including inmates in jail or prison) beyond the scheduled time for the interview. Similarly, when study participants are adolescents participating with the permission of their parents who are waiting to take them home, additional consideration is called for. In these cases, the interviewer should clarify whether it is appropriate to communicate with the client's parent, counselor, or corrections officer and take responsibility (i.e., apologize) for detaining or keeping the individual, client, or inmate for a longer time than earlier anticipated. Again, such considerations are part and parcel of maintaining ongoing support for the project as a whole. Taking these additional measures after an interview communicates that the interviewers are aware that they may have crossed established (power) boundaries and simultaneously reestablishes the integrity of these institutional or custodial boundaries.

In a similar way, the interviewer can return the participant to her or his "usual self" after the interview is completed. By making small talk, discussing plans for the rest of the day, answering

participants' questions about the project, or expressing appreciation for having met the participant, interviewers can help participants shift from the interview to the rest of the day. However,
participants are sometimes reluctant to return to their everyday
activities, especially when these occur in any range of unpleasant
settings. It is best to conclude and move on from the contact
within five minutes of closing the interview, even if this is socially
difficult. Otherwise, it is likely that interviewers will voluntarily
shift into or feel pressured to adopt any number of other roles
(e.g., therapist, case worker, teacher, preacher, job coach, family
member, even corrections officer) that are beyond the scope of
their role as interviewers.

## LOGISTICS

Interviews in the field are often costly in time and other resources,
whether they are conducted in a storefront or elsewhere in the interviewee's community. The interviewer must travel to the site, which
sometimes requires a considerable allocation of time. Those in
high-risk populations, however, are often unable or unwilling to
travel to a site to participate in the interview, so the interviewer
must go to them. In fact, it is often the only way to gain information about these groups.

Scheduling and following through on actually conducting the
interview provide unique challenges in high-risk populations.
Homelessness is not unusual, and place of residence changes frequently. Many do not maintain working and consistent phone
numbers; many have aliases. Sometimes an appointment is set
for an interview, and the interviewee does not appear at the
appointed time. It is frequently difficult to get in touch with the
person to reschedule the interview. Although it is often useful to
provide an incentive for the person to be interviewed, this far from
guarantees that the person will actually appear for the interview.
Resource budgeting should take into account the reality of no
shows at interviews.

Managing field data collection requires realistic expectations about reaching populations that are hard to reach, strategies for how to handle no shows, doing everything possible to ensure interviewer safety, and keeping communication open and frequent with the interviewers. This is in addition to concern for the quality of the information being gathered.

As we mentioned earlier, consistency in the way questions are asked and responses are coded is a key concern, especiall when more than one interviewer is conducting the interviews. To a lesser extent, this issue about consistency arises even if a single interviewer conducts all the interviews. Analyses of the information gathered begin with the assumption that the information reflects true and accurate responses by those being questioned, as well as consistent responses, no matter who is conducting the interview and on what day. If this is not the case, the responses are truly limited in their usefulness, are not likely to answer the questions the interview was designed to address, and will make comparisons across interviews difficult. To better ensure consistency in interview procedures across several interviewers, and preferably under the guidance of management, the interviewers should meet periodically to review established criteria for conducting interviews, especially on difficult or ambiguous topics. Clearly, consistency is an issue, whether interviews are conducted in the field or in a facility. Conditions in the field, however, often make it harder to focus on these issues than on the multitude of distractions and safety issues that occur there.

## CONCLUSION

In closing, keep in mind that obtaining information from interviews is just the beginning of learning about the subject of interest. The information has to be analyzed, and reports that summarize the findings usually have to be written. These topics—interview, analysis, and writing—represent the full circle of gathering important information from another person.

## SUGGESTED READINGS

Bernard, H. R. (1995). *Research methods in anthropology: Qualitative and quantitative approaches.* Walnut Creek, CA: Altamira Press.

Coulehan, J. L., & Block, M. R. (1997). *The medical interview: Mastering skills for clinical practice.* Philadelphia: F. A. Davis.

Rossi, P. H., Wright, J. D., & Anderson, A. B. (1983). *Handbook of survey research.* San Diego: Academic Press.

# 3

# FOLLOW-UP AND TRACKING METHODS FOR HARD-TO-REACH POPULATIONS

**KRISTINE ZIEK, B.A., NELSON TIBURCIO, M.A., and NADINA CORREA**

Follow-up is a vital component of many research and service efforts. Research studies follow up program participants to assess behavioral trends and the effectiveness and impact of interventions over time. If measurements are to be accurate, research subjects must be retained throughout the project. Service organizations follow clients to provide effective care for many types of illnesses and services, such as therapies for tuberculosis, vaccines for hepatitis B, or the tracking of welfare participants who enter the workforce. The major difference between follow-up in research and follow-up in service programs is that research subjects are typically recruited into a project, whereas many participants tend to seek out service providers themselves. This difference often has an impact on participants' motivation to maintain contact with the program, which is an important factor in successful follow-up.

In this chapter, we describe the techniques that we have found most useful in the follow-up of research and service clients, and we illustrate the steps we have taken to effectively conduct follow-ups. Our techniques are divided into standard procedures (basic, cost-effective techniques), enhanced procedures (labor-intensive procedures we use when standard procedures do not work), and measures used in extreme situations, when neither standard nor enhanced procedures are effective. We illustrate these procedures with examples from our own field-based research. Throughout the chapter, we use the word *client* or *subject* to refer to participants in the projects we describe.

## COMMON CHALLENGES TO EFFECTIVE FOLLOW-UP AND STRATEGIES TO MEET THESE CHALLENGES

People at the margins of society are difficult to locate for many reasons. The lack of a telephone or a permanent address is usually the first obstacle. Each specific subpopulation presents its own unique set of obstacles. For habitual drug users, aspects of their lifestyle make it difficult to keep up their participation in a program. Those involved in illegal activity—in many cases, their only means of financial support—are often forced into hiding. Criminal activity and active drug use may cause estrangement from families and friends, leading to unstable living arrangements. Homelessness among many disenfranchised populations is also a growing problem, especially in urban areas. Overcrowded and unsafe shelters make many who have lost their housing feel that living on the street is their only option. Once on the streets, these individuals become extremely difficult to locate. The mentally ill can be hard to follow for multiple reasons: higher rates of homelessness, the active symptoms of mental illness, and the limited ability of the treatment system to meet the needs of these individuals. Recovering substance abusers also present unique follow-up problems. In many instances, recovering persons dissociate themselves from the past, including the organizations that provided treatment and services to aid in their recovery. If a project's staff, office, or clientele represents a "trigger" to a recovering substance abuser, there can be an inherent conflict between participation and maintaining recovery. For many, across all these subgroups, there is a lack of trust in research and service organizations, some of which may be justifiable, but this distrust can make follow-up very difficult and needs to be addressed.

Although some of these issues may be readily apparent, each population is likely to present additional obstacles to successful follow-up. Whenever possible, it is most important to identify these issues before beginning follow-up activities. One method for discovering these issues is through focus groups, which can provide concrete strategies for improving follow-up rates. For instance, focus groups for one project dealing with methadone maintenance dropouts revealed that identifying the project as a "health study" was undesirable because many participants in the groups felt that "health study" implied the possibility of HIV infection or other stigmatized health problems. A community or neighborhood "survey" was more acceptable to this population, and follow-up protocols were worded accordingly. Mentally ill participants, however, may prefer "health study," which conveys a more neutral context than the stigma associated with mental illness. Focus groups allow direct interaction with the population being followed in order to understand its particular concerns.

Protocols should be established early in the project. In this way, follow-up procedures can be incorporated into all aspects of program planning. For example, clients can be told at their initial contact that follow-up will occur and when and how it will take place (e.g., with a telephone interview 3 months from intake or with a scheduled office visit in 6 months). In many cases, follow-up occurs as part of ongoing treatment planning and scheduling, but making the follow-up procedures explicit and concrete for all clients fosters high follow-up rates. Based on feedback from clients, reevaluate methods regularly and be willing to change them if they are not working.

Early planning also helps staff anticipate the needs of the project when it comes to follow-up. The resources devoted to follow-up depend on the importance placed on reaching most or all clients. For instance, follow-up is very important in research on tuberculosis and other infectious diseases and less important for routine health surveys or one-shot interventions such as immunizations. Keeping this in mind enables a project to budget appropriately for the type of follow-up that meets its requirements. Staffing needs for conducting follow-up activities should be well defined when budgets and long-term goals are developed. Including the harder-to-find clients in a project requires devoting considerably more time to locating them. For example, if a program decides to follow active drug users, as in the projects we have worked on, a week may be required for tracking the stable portion of the population and a month for tracking the less stable part of the population. Follow-up requires staff involvement from the start of the project, and this involvement increases as time goes on. Projects already working in the field may have to consider hiring additional staff to implement an effective follow-up.

Staff–client interactions during assessment and/or intake, treatment, and attempts to make contact for follow-up can have an enormous impact on follow-up rates (see the chapters on outreach and interviewing for discussions of how to maximize the success of these activities). A project must develop an atmosphere of mutual respect and professionalism to engage people at intake and expect them to want to return. Much of the success of the follow-up derives from the special skills of staff members. Examples include knowledge of drug use (e.g., drug street names, drug classification, and modes of ingestion), an overall street savvy, and an ability to engage disenfranchised clients in difficult situations. Our clients report that this engagement and understanding are major factors in their decisions to continue participating in all phases of our projects, including follow-up.

Because much follow-up takes place outside established institutional and residential settings, establishing a street and community presence is important. Building trust and rapport with the community greatly facilitates a project's street-based follow-up activities. When a community understands and respects a project, members of the community have a positive view of the project's activities and can sometimes act as "eyes on the street" when you are looking for a specific hard-to-reach individual. Building an ongoing relationship with the community in which the project operates and fostering cooperation with community members and other community organizations enhance any follow-up effort.

Many follow-up activities require the cooperation of institutions to be successful. For example, projects may wish to follow clients who are in jail, a hospital, or receiving treatment in a residential facility, depending on how important follow-up is to the success of the project. It is important to begin relationships with institutions far in advance, in that the process of building these institutional linkages can be time-consuming and unpredictable. By establishing these associations early in the project, staff can avoid situations in which the opportunity to follow clients at a specific time is lost because of delays in gaining access to institutions. In addition to formal agreements with institutions, presentations of project goals and introduction of project staff members should be made to institutional staff as part of the linkage process. These presentations should focus on the specific protocols to be used, the sharing (or lack of sharing) of information, and the overall aims of the project. By focusing on institutional staff as well as on the institution itself, follow-up contact with clients is more likely to be facilitated.

The following sections cover specific protocols and tracking methods for following hard-to-reach populations. We present both the standard and enhanced follow-up techniques, as well as some specific strategies for dealing with extreme situations.

## STANDARD PROCEDURES

Standard procedures are used in most, if not all, follow-up activities. They represent the basic components of any follow-up protocol and capture the easiest-to-reach members of hard-to-reach populations. At the beginning of a project, it is important to define the specific criteria for follow-up. For example, will there be more than one follow-up? When will each follow-up take place (e.g., three months and six months after baseline, or will there be only one follow-up)? How long before the follow-up is scheduled should staff begin to contact clients? Should there be a maximum time after which follow-up would no longer be considered? How should clients be contacted (e.g., phone, mail, e-mail, outreach)? The answers to these questions will be based on clinical and research concerns, as well as resource allocation considerations. Once these and other decisions have been made, a system should be implemented to ensure that people due for follow-up will be contacted in a timely matter. If possible, computer software should be used to create a contact database that will help in all aspects of follow-up. If electronic technology is beyond the budget of a project, records can be maintained by hand.

## Using Computer Software

A computer database aids in organizing mailings, maintaining accurate and up-to-date information, and producing lists that can be used for matching names during searches of institutional databases. It is also a helpful tool in recording comments related to locating clients; these comments can be reviewed and used to adapt follow-up protocols. The decision to use the computer for each of these applications should be based on the size of the staff, the number of follow-ups required for the project, and the resources available to the organization. In many different settings, databases are used widely for client tracking, billing, and scheduling. These databases, designed for commercial use, can be easily adapted to facilitate follow-up tracking. Alternatively, separate follow-up databases can be developed and then linked to master client databases. Excel, Access, Filemaker Pro, and Visual FoxPro are common software packages that can be used for these purposes. Other useful software includes Symantec ACT! 4.0, Maximizer 5.0, and Gold-Mine 4.0.

## Developing a Locator Form

Projects often use a printed form to collect information used in contacting the clients for follow-up interviews. We call this document a locator form. These forms must be as comprehensive as possible and include items specific to the population being followed. For example, space should be allowed to record soup kitchens frequented by the homeless, needle exchanges used by injection drug users, or 12-step programs attended by recovering addicts. This information is collected at intake and updated at subsequent visits. The more information that is collected, the more likely it is that the client can be contacted for follow-up. Most clients will probably be reached through the most basic information on the locator form (telephone number and address). Because the staff cannot know beforehand which clients will be easy to contact, however, locator forms must be collected from everyone to make sure that information is available for those clients who turn out to be especially hard to reach. To develop a locator form, keep in mind that different subsets of information can be used for different populations and that many organizations have this information stored in other forms where it can easily be gathered if needed (e.g., information stored in medical records, billing records, and client databases). Maintaining the accuracy of the locator information is crucial to the follow-up process. All relevant information regarding the client should be noted, including any information the client shares regarding future plans or current situation (e.g., travel, moving, possible court dates, and pregnancy).

These locator forms are considered a confidential part of a client's file or chart, and this information cannot be released without the client's explicit consent. Thus, information about institutions the client accesses can be used to inform outreach activities, but clients cannot be contacted through a specific institution unless they have authorized this type of contact. In the research projects we have worked on, the locator forms are shredded before being disposed of at the end of the funding period.

Some sample items that are part of the locator forms we use include full name (including maiden name), nicknames or street names, social security number, public assistance ID number, current mailing address, telephone number, beeper number, and e-mail address. We also ask clients for the identification we should use when telephoning, addresses and/or telephone numbers of friends and relatives who would be able to contact the client, addresses and/or telephone numbers of a counselor or parole officer who would be able to contact the subject, hangout areas (include seasonal hangouts), place and time the subject met the outreach team, and a photo or physical description of the subject. A sample locator form from one of our projects is reproduced in the appendix following this chapter. Note that our information is specific to our client population (in this case, a research sample of out-of-treatment drug injectors), that other projects would most likely have somewhat different forms, and that our form is very lengthy because we conduct research projects in which the follow-up component is crucial to our research design. Thus, we must devote significant resources to tracking and locating hard-to-reach subjects. Again, individual projects allocate resources according to their needs and develop locator forms and tracking protocols based on these decisions.

In collecting locator information, acquire more than one address and phone number if possible. Sometimes, getting even one is difficult. To encourage clients to provide this information, it is helpful to give them a sense of what will be said to someone who answers the phone or receives the mail. Having a sample of the letter to be mailed out before follow-up can allay some fears. In a project in which clients are focusing on intimate or stigmatized behaviors, such as drug use and sexual behavior, they must trust the project staff enough to give the addresses and phone numbers of friends and family.

Updating information at each subsequent meeting is also important. Any additional information obtained from subsequent meetings with a client should be recorded; for example, we make note of new addresses and phone numbers, recent marriages and divorces, and entrance into residential drug treatment. In addition, information should be updated when attempts to contact clients reveal that the information has changed (e.g., a letter is forwarded, a phone number is disconnected, family or friends indicate that a client now lives or hangs out somewhere else). Because many clients lead unstable lives, with frequent shifts in living situations, updating locator forms is critical to the ongoing success of follow-up.

When contacting clients directly does not succeed, often other family members, neighbors, or friends can be reached. These people tend to be protective of clients, especially when their behavior is illegal or stigmatized. Therefore, initial reactions to anyone inquiring about these clients can include "I do not know him," "What do you want from him?" or "I am tired of bailing him out." An unthreatening matter-of-fact attitude usually gets a positive response from friends and family. Clients can assist in developing these strategies during the session when locator information is collected.

## Appointment Cards and Phone Calls

Appointment cards are a useful way to remind clients about future appointments. The content of the card needs to be considered carefully because the cards may be seen by family members and others. Typically, identifying information about the client would not be included on the card, and the text on the card should be neutral, revealing little specific information about the client or the project. Usually, a date, a time, and an acronym identifying the project suffice.

Before making calls, review the locator form for specific instructions regarding whom to ask for, how to identify the caller, and what kind of messages can be left. It is never advisable to mention anything that may embarrass the client or compromise promises of confidentiality, and it is generally a good idea to provide as little information as possible about the project to whoever answers the phone. Most calls will be routine; the person answering the phone will not ask any questions and will take a message for the client. However, if the message taker makes inquiries and is suspicious of the caller or the project, the primary obligation is to protect the client's privacy.

Establishing an 800 phone line or accepting collect calls can be a cost-effective way of maintaining contact with clients, as it allows clients without phones to stay in contact with the project and allows them to make contact even if they are not at their own phones. If possible, a phone number that incorporates the project's name or a memorable phrase (e.g., 1-800-HEALTHY) will help participants remember how to get in touch even if they lose the project business cards. Keep in mind that some prisons do not allow inmates to use 800 lines; if clients are likely to be in jail or prison, they can be encouraged to make collect calls to stay in touch with the project.

## Keeping in Touch Before Follow-Up Is Due

Sending a letter is an extremely cost-effective way of maintaining contact with clients. In most cases, letters reminding clients that they are scheduled for follow-up should be sent a few weeks before the client is due at the office. The contents of the letter will vary depending on the specifics of each project, but generally these letters should remind clients of their participation in the project, explain that it is time to schedule a follow-up interview, and invite clients to contact the project in person or by phone to set up the appointment. If a follow-up was scheduled previously (e.g., at the last contact), the letter can remind clients of the scheduled appointment and invite them to contact the project if there is a problem with the scheduled time. Any special circumstances can be outlined in the letter (e.g., clients will receive a stipend for participating in follow-up or clients should fast because blood will be drawn at the next visit). As with any client contact, participants should be informed at intake that follow-up letters will be sent and should be told that they have the right to request that letters not be sent if they are concerned about lack of confidentiality. In general, the majority of clients in our projects who return for the follow-up interview return within two months of the initial mailing. When no response to the initial mailing occurs within the first two weeks, letters are mailed to all the additional contact addresses listed, and a phone call is made to the client.

In addition to reminding clients about follow-up appointments, letters and cards can be used to maintain contact, promote clients' positive feelings toward the project, and provide a brief reminder that a follow-up is expected in the future. In projects that require multiple contacts, maintaining regular contact over time will increase the likelihood that clients can be located when follow-up is due. Sending birthday cards and holiday cards is one way to do this. Sending thank-you notes after each interview is also an effective way to maintain contact. A project newsletter is another way to stay in touch, as long as participation in the project is not something the client wishes to keep private (e.g., a newsletter for a childhood asthma initiative may help to maintain contact with clients, but one for an HIV prevention project may not be appropriate without clients' consent).

By sending mail regularly, the project will be informed when addresses are no longer valid. The first time that any letter is returned, the mailing address should be compared to the locator form to ensure that the letter was addressed properly. The telephone directory can provide an additional check for accuracy of addresses. If a forwarding address sticker has been placed on the envelope by the post office, the new information should be transferred to the database and the letter sent again. When the post office returns a letter twice for the *same reason,* the address should then be considered invalid. All returned letters should be recorded in the database, citing the reason for return, the date of new mailing, and other comments regarding efforts made to locate the participant.

## ENHANCED PROCEDURES

The following sections illustrate procedures that can be used when the standard follow-up procedures just discussed are ineffective. In general, these "enhanced" procedures are more labor-intensive but also more likely to succeed with clients who are more difficult to follow.

## Missed Appointments and Walk-Ins

Most service and research settings rely on scheduled appointments to accomplish their work efficiently. Unfortunately, many clients miss scheduled appointments, leading to staff frustration and a waste of resources. Although it is virtually impossible to guarantee perfect attendance by all clients, some steps can be taken to minimize this problem. Confirmation of an appointment can be made the day before for those who have phones. If an appointment is made more than a week in advance, a reminder can be mailed. If an outreach team is in the field, clients can be visited. Additional strategies can limit the impact of missed appointments. Projects can overbook appointment times (e.g., schedule three appointments at a time when staff are available to see only two clients, or schedule appointments every 30 minutes for a follow-up protocol that requires 45 minutes to conduct). By overbooking, some clients may be forced to wait for their scheduled appointment, but staff time will be used more efficiently. It is also possible to schedule home or off-site interviews, where the no-show rate is likely to be lower. In any of these situations, projects must make a trade-off between client convenience and staff resources.

Clients can also be late to appointments for many reasons. It is advisable to allow a short period of time, such as half an hour, before making a call to the client. It is good strategy to be as understanding as possible about the first missed appointment and to accommodate the client as much as possible. Ask the client when the best time would be to reschedule, or be willing to see the late client. When missed or late appointments become common for a particular client, the issue should be addressed with the goal of finding a mutually acceptable time for future appointments (e.g., sending a car service or scheduling the appointment immediately following other appointments the client keeps, such as treatment groups or work).

Clients who are uncomfortable about setting appointments in advance can be encouraged to walk in on their own when they are due for a follow-up. When clients do walk in for an unscheduled appointment, they usually want to be seen on the spot; if walk-ins are accepted, they should be seen as quickly as possible to make sure that they are retained and to increase the likelihood that they will return for future contacts. In our experience, many participants walk out if they do not feel they are being treated properly. This means that staff must be ready to perform extra unscheduled sessions at all times. Like many other aspects of follow-up, the decision to devote resources to walk-ins is based on how valuable follow-up is to the project.

## Follow-Up Conducted Outside the Office

In some cases, clients do not want to come to the office, although they are willing to participate in follow-up. Sometimes clients view the office as a stigmatizing place where they would prefer not to be seen, such as an AIDS treatment clinic. In other cases, clients may be physically unable to reach the office because of a physical challenge or because they live far away. Recovering substance abusers may view the office, the other clients, or the area in which the project is located as potential relapse triggers. Many projects still wish to follow these clients. In these situations, other arrangements can be made. Many projects now conduct a portion of their work in the community by using outreach staff and mobile vans. In other situations, interviews, although not treatment, can be conducted in noninstitutional settings, such as at a coffee shop or in a park. Clients may also be willing to visit alternative institutional settings (e.g., an AIDS clinic located in a different neighborhood). Finally, some projects conduct follow-up activities in clients' homes. Although this can be logistically difficult and time-consuming, visits to clients' homes provide a unique insight into their lives that can have important service and research implications.

## Telephone Follow-Up

In some cases, face-to-face follow-up is impossible. For example, clients may have moved out of state or may be in a correctional facility in a different part of the state. Some clients may simply be unwilling to come in or meet with project staff directly. In these situations, the only remaining option may be to conduct follow-up activities by telephone. Some follow-up activities are impossible over the telephone (e.g., detailed medical examinations, blood or urine testing), and others are compromised (e.g., the quality of interview information), but some useful data will be recorded; these data may be preferable to either losing contact with the client or taking on costly expenses to locate and visit the client. The most important aspect of telephone follow-up is recognizing its limitations and making any accommodations possible to address these limitations. Telephone interviewers should be trained to distinguish subtleties of voice and to use specific probing methods to elicit more valid information. Clients can be trained in advance to gather and record basic medical information by using home health kits (e.g., blood pressure monitors, glucose tests) and can then provide this information over the telephone. Although telephone contact involves some compromises, it is likely that medical and social service providers will increasingly rely on this type of follow-up, which may prove to be extremely cost-effective.

## EXTREME SITUATIONS

This section focuses on situations in which clients cannot be followed up. Even though these clients are "lost" at this point, and no follow-up is possible, some strategies can still benefit both the client and the project.

After project staff have made their best efforts to meet with a client, the client may not be interested in returning to the project. Although this can occur for many reasons, there are few options available for project staff. Any contact with the client should focus on obtaining any follow-up data possible and on uncovering reasons for the refusal to participate. The client who changes his or her mind and is willing to come in or otherwise participate in follow-up should be accommodated. Under no circumstances should interviewers try to force clients to return. This point may seem obvious, but in practice it is difficult to determine the boundary between encouraging participation and subtle coercion. In general, project staff can speak with clients to get a good sense of why they are refusing to return and try to make them understand the importance of their own particular role in the project. By doing this with all clients who refuse to return, a project can gather information that improves retention rates in the future and communicates the message that a client's wishes are respected.

If all attempts to get the client back fail, it is important to end the relationship on a positive note. Thank the client for listening and for participating in the project. Be understanding and non-judgmental so that the door is left open for future participation. Even if people refuse to participate in follow-up, it is important to leave them with a positive impression of the project and institution, so that they may feel comfortable reestablishing contact at a later date. Invite clients to call back if they reconsider. The following scenario illustrates one such case in one of our research projects:

> After no response to the follow-up form letter, a call was made to the client. After two or three unsuccessful attempts, a contact was finally made by phone. The client revealed that he no longer was "in the scene" and really wasn't interested in being part of the study. The next day the follow-up coordinator called and, through a series of negotiations, offered to have one of the staff meet the client off-site. The client said that this would be all right but that it was not a good time to talk and asked that they continue the conversation the next day. When the follow-up coordinator returned the call, he had changed his mind. The client said that he wasn't really happy with the experience. After some discussion and attempts to smooth things out, the client remained adamant about not returning. The conversation ended pleasantly with the follow-up coordinator saying that the door was always open if the client should have a change of heart. Two months later the client walked into the field site and completed the interview.

## ENHANCED METHODS

### Street Tracking, Social Networks, and Institutional Searches

Street tracking is a very expensive proposition that is likely to be conducted only when follow-up is essential, when multiple projects pool resources, or when the population is solely (or at least primarily) a street-based population. Part of street tracking is having the street presence mentioned in Chapter 1. Once the outreach staff is known in the community, street tracking becomes much easier. To maintain rapport with clients and the community, it is important to have outreach staff in the field regularly. While in the field, the team may see clients repeatedly. At times, clients may disappear from the streets. For many clients, circumstances can change dramatically in a short time. People get arrested, pass away, or move out of the community. In our projects, frequenting popular subway stations, indoor and outdoor shooting galleries, drug "copping spots," prostitution "strolls," and panhandling areas helps the outreach workers keep in touch with what is happening on the street. With the client's prior permission (usually obtained at intake), the outreach team can ask their street contacts for information when they are trying to locate a particular client. The following example illustrates the success of networking with the community:

> One of our clients could not be found. The mailings were all delivered to the addresses on the locator. Messages were left for the client at the only phone number provided on the locator. The woman at the other end of the phone seemed surprised that we had seen the client but gave us no other information. A member of the outreach team later heard through her street contacts that the client was in a residential treatment center. A call was made to the client at the center. After permission was obtained from the center, an interviewer was sent over and the interview was conducted.

Without a sustained and trusted presence on the street, the outreach team would seldom be in the position to learn the location of project clients.

Institutional information systems (databases) and service providers can be good sources of locating information. Obtaining permission to use institutional information systems can be time-consuming and labor-intensive. For example, gaining access to the Shelter Care Information Management Systems in New York City requires approval from multiple agencies and typically takes months. Projects should be prepared to spend extended periods gaining access to institutions such as hospitals and local departments of health. Because of this time lag, it is important to begin this process early in the project, rather than initiating it during the follow-up stage to track particular clients who are not returning. Sometimes, through networking within these institutions, it is possible to find more direct sources of information, such as clinicians, case workers, or outreach workers, and save valuable time. Some institutions now allow Internet access to their databases for authorized users. In some cases, government or other institutions can provide assistance in locating current addresses and telephone numbers or information on whether specific individuals have recently passed away. Table 3-1 lists these institutions.

Once a client is located in an institution, a project can decide

**TABLE 3-1    List of Institutions That May Provide Locator Information**

*Local health departments:* Death records

*Telephone company:* Current addresses and phone numbers

*Motor vehicles:* Current addresses

*Human services:* Current addresses

*Shelter system:* Current address

*Prison system:* Locating/possible interview

*National Death Index (NDI),* Hyattsville, Maryland (301-436-8951): A costly but effective way of gathering information about deaths in the United States, including Puerto Rico and the Virgin Islands. The information is about 11 to 12 months behind.

whether to take the steps necessary to complete a follow-up interview. This decision is again based on the importance of each specific follow-up contact and the resources required to make this contact (e.g., the cost in transportation and staff time). In many cases, clients may be institutionalized but willing to be interviewed. Once it is determined that interviews are to be conducted within an institution, such as a hospital, drug treatment facility, or prison, a (hopefully) preexisting system for gaining access to clients within the institution can be put into place. Ease of access varies from institution to institution, and between facilities within the same institution. For example, some jails or prisons are easier to access than others. In New York City, the municipal jails are much easier to access than the state prison system, and therefore our projects try to locate clients as soon as they are arrested and before they are sent to an upstate prison or to other jurisdictions. It pays to know the local correctional system, as well as other institutional systems, and how to access information regarding clients in these institutions.

It is not always as easy to conduct an on-site institutional interview as it might seem. Traveling to institutions is time-consuming, even when these institutions are local. Once at an institution, it is often necessary to wait for clients or interview space to become available. Clients may also decline to participate in the follow-up at the last minute; this risk can be minimized by having the follow-up conducted by a staff person who has had prior contact with the client. If a client is to be paid for the interview (as is common in research), special accommodations must sometimes be made for the client in a residential facility or prison, where it may not be permissible to carry cash. Medical or biological testing (e.g., HIV testing, urinalysis) may also be difficult to carry out in some institutions. It is advisable to find out the policies of specific institutions in advance, so that the project can decide if, and how, to carry out institution-based follow-up.

Some institutions, such as drug treatment programs and shelters, may not allow contact with their clients because of issues of client confidentiality. In the case of shelters, visiting can be useful even if direct access to clients is prohibited. Information about when clients leave and return can be obtained directly from the shelter or by the outreach team on the streets; many shelters do not allow clients to stay during the day. Of course, in these situations special care must be taken in approaching clients because discussing the project with them publicly could violate their confidentiality. As a general rule, staff should never talk to clients about their participation within earshot of others because clients may not want others to know they are part of the project. If outreach is to be used to reach clients for follow-up, the specific outreach protocols should be discussed with clients at intake, when contact information is gathered.

Another good source for locating hard-to-find clients is what we to refer to as "help networks," which help clients obtain services. Clients may seek (1) drug detoxification, (2) access to mental health services, (3) economic help (e.g., welfare, Social Security), (4) physical health care, or (5) legal aid. It is helpful to spend time getting to know providers in these areas. Clients often provide the names of case managers, social workers, and other professionals as part of their contact information. Establishing a liaison with these professionals can prove to be useful for trying to reach clients. Visiting soup kitchens at meal times may also be useful in locating hard-to-find clients. Again, staff must be careful about confidentiality in these situations.

Persistence and tenacity usually win out in the field. Often, the conditions under which clients are contacted in the street do not allow the client to make an appointment on the spot or to go directly back to an office to participate in follow-up. Sometimes it takes many street contacts to succeed in getting the client back to the office. Keep in mind that this type of tracking is very labor-intensive and therefore is used only when contacting clients for follow-up is essential and worth the extra investment in resources.

The following is an example of an intensive tracking effort on one of our projects:

A client left a therapeutic community (TC) in October 1995, with no follow-up information provided to the clinical staff. The only useful information was that the client left without his medication. We first reviewed the client's locator form for contact information about "significant others." Unfortunately, the locator form provided no information about significant others because the client refused to supply us with any names. A check of the client's clinical records revealed that he also refused to provide our counselors with any previous addresses or similar data. The only useful information in the client's clinical record was the institution from which he was referred. After speaking to the social worker who made the original referral, it was determined that the client had not been back and had refused to give any information about his family. On a hunch, and having noted that the client left without his medication, we checked the self-reported hospitalization history and contacted each of the hospitals listed. We found that the client had been treated in a hospital emergency room two nights before for psychiatric destabilization. We were informed that the client had an appointment with the benefits administrator the next day (benefits appointments are *rarely* missed). An interviewer went to the hospital and was there waiting to speak to the client when he kept his benefits appointment.

This example illustrates the investigative effort that sometimes must be made to locate clients when they "disappear." Ongoing discussions among project staff regarding strategies can help to formulate new strategies. This example also illustrates why accurate and detailed record keeping is so important; seemingly irrelevant parts of the client's record were instrumental in locating him for follow-up.

## Other Impediments to Follow-Up

Sometimes a client is contacted but has no recollection of the project. Mentioning the interviewer's name and the date that the latest interview took place can help. Before discussing anything specific about the project, it is essential to be certain that the person you are talking to is, in fact, the person whom you seek. Compare the birth date and Social Security number to project records to make sure. Try to ask some basic demographic questions and compare the answers to the information you already have. Some clients may resist providing personal information over the phone. A good approach is to let the person know that the questions are asked to protect them. For example, the staff person may say, "Before we go any further, I need to confirm that you were interviewed with us before. It is our way of protecting your privacy. Could you please give me your birth date and Social Security number?" Ultimately, if the client's identity is still uncertain after these questions have been asked, it is best to explain that any further discussion or questions regarding the study will be answered at the interview.

In some cases, direct contact with a client is impossible, and third parties must be contacted to locate the client. In these cases, even though the client has provided contact information for the third parties, it is important to maintain client confidentiality. The following paragraphs illustrate some common challenges to maintaining client confidentiality in these circumstances.

## CONFIDENTIALITY ISSUES

If clients are no longer reachable at the telephone number they provided, follow-up staff may want the person on the other end of the phone to relay a message or give a number where the client can be reached. In this situation, maintaining confidentiality is essential and sometimes tricky. As with other types of third-party contacts, this procedure should be reviewed with the client at intake, and the locator should have specific instructions for handling these phone calls, including procedures for leaving messages.

Sometimes other people or agencies will contact a project looking for a client. In these cases, it is again essential to maintain the confidentiality of each client. It is generally not permissible to give out information about any client to *anyone* outside the project staff. In some cases, with the client's written permission, it is permissible to share information. For example, a client may wish to list the project as a contact for a treatment program or request the project to furnish information to a service provider. In these cases, it is necessary to document that the client has requested this and to verify that the information is being provided to the person or agency the client has designated. In other cases, clients may include a project they have regular contact with on the locator used in another project. In these cases, it is important to check with clients to determine that they would like to be contacted this way. Many of our projects respond to these requests by stating that they cannot provide any information about clients without written permission. They may then, however, inform the client of this contact at the next appointment.

When inquiring about clients, take care not to raise suspicion. Keep the tone as matter-of-fact as possible. The aim is to explain the project simply and clearly. Scripts should be prepared and rehearsed ahead of time, and they should be reviewed by clients as part of the discussion of follow-up contact that takes place at intake. Our experience has shown that if the word *confidential* is used right away, people react very suspiciously. The explanation you provide should be as simple as possible to avoid the possibility of tension. The key is to reveal as little information as possible while at the same time getting as much information as possible. The following is an example of a script we use in our research projects:

Hello. This is _____ from the Neighborhood Survey. May I
       speak to _____.

*He's not here right now.*

Can I please leave a message? Ask _____ to call
       _____ at _____.

*What kind of survey is this?*

It's a survey of community needs. Could you please tell
_____ we called?

*What kind of needs are you talking about?*

I am sorry but I really am not allowed to discuss the details of the
survey with anybody but the people involved in the survey.

*Why?*

We promise all the participants confidentiality. Could you please
tell _____ I called? My name is _____ at the
Neighborhood Survey, and my number is _____.
Thank you.

Although there is no guarantee that a client will get the message
after an interaction such as this, the client's confidentiality remains
secure.

## CONCLUSION

Following up hard-to-reach clients, although difficult, is usually
possible, as this chapter has illustrated. Often, the success of
these efforts reflects the resources allocated to them. Individual
projects must decide how to spend their resources based on how
important follow-up contact is to them. In these cases, the project
truly does get what it pays for. A full-time staff devoted to tracking
and locating clients will increase follow-up. Even with careful
planning, a high follow-up rate is difficult to achieve with
hard-to-reach populations. Frustration is inevitable and can be
addressed by regular staff discussions and problem-solving sessions. When follow-up is treated as an important part of a project,
both staff enthusiasm and actual rates of follow-up will increase. A
project that is flexible, ready to reevaluate its methods, and able to
adapt new protocols when necessary will find its follow-up efforts
well rewarded.

## SUGGESTED READINGS

Anglin, M. D., Danila, B., Ryan, T., & Mantius, K. (1996). *Staying in touch: A fieldwork manual of tracking procedures for locating substance abusers for follow-up studies.* Fairfax, VA: National Evaluation Data and Technical Assistance Center (NEDTAC).

Goldstein, P. J., Abbott, W., Paige, W., & Sobel, I. T. (1977). Tracking procedures in follow-up studies of drug abusers. *American Journal of Drug & Alcohol Abuse, 4* (1), 21–30.

Hindmand, K., & Jainchill, N. *Interviewer guidelines/procedures for conducting post-treatment (follow-up) interviews.* New York: Center for Therapeutic Community Research, NDRI.

Nurco, D. N. (1991). *Follow-up fieldwork: AIDS outreach and IV drug abuse* (DHHS Publication No. Adm 92-1884). Rockville, MD: National Institute on Drug Abuse.

Ziek, K., Beardsley, M., Deren, S., & Tortu, S. (1996). Predictors of follow-up in a sample of urban crack users. *Evaluation and Program Planning, 19* (3), 219–224.

## APPENDIX: SAMPLE LOCATOR FOR
## DRUG USERS WITH FEW ADDRESSES

Interview Date: _ _ / _ _ / _ _

Client ID# _ _

Interviewer ID# _ _

Respondent birth date: _ _ / _ _ / _ _

*Interviewer read:* Within the next few months we will be contacting you again. You can help us now by giving me some information on how best to contact you. None of the information you give us will be associated with your answers in our interview. Your name and other information will be linked to a unique number and kept confidential in a locked file, separate from the file in which the interview form is kept. It will not be given to anyone outside our research staff, and the information will be destroyed after completion of the interviewing phase. It is important that the information you give us is accurate. If there is a question you do not want to answer, it would be better to tell us that you do not want to answer the question, rather than giving us incorrect information. If we speak to anyone when trying to locate you, we will say that we are from the Community Survey.

1. First, please tell me your *full* name:

   _____  _____  _____  (_____)
   (FIRST)               (MIDDLE)             (LAST)              (MAIDEN,
                                                                                  IF FEMALE)

2. What other names, street names,
   nicknames, or aliases do you go by?      1 = none

   _____       _____       _____

3. Could you please provide us with your Social Security number?
   _ _ _ ‾ _ _ ‾ _ _ _ _

4. Could you provide us with your public assistance ID number?
   _____

   Name of agency _____

5. Could you provide us with your driver's license number?
   _____

   State of issue: _____

6. You will be paid $20.00 for your next interview. When we want to contact you to schedule that interview, we will need the following information:

   **Home address:**

   c/o Name: _____ Relationship: _____

   Street:_____ Apt # _____

   City: _____ State: _____ Zip code: _____

Is this address a shelter?  1 = Yes **If yes:** Bed # _____ ID # _____

0 = No

**Mailing address:**          1 = same as above

c/o Name: _____ Relationship: _____

Street:_____ Apt # _____

City: _____ State: _____ Zip code: _____

Is this address a shelter?  1 = Yes **If yes:** Bed # _____ ID # _____

0 = No

7. At which of these addresses are you currently living?

   1 = Home address, 2 = Mailing address

   Can we visit you at this address?        1 = Yes, 0 = No

   Day _____ Time _____

   What are the cross streets to this address?

   1. _____

   2. _____

   What train and/or bus would you take to this address?

   _____

   Call first?        1 = Yes        0 = No

8. What is your phone number or beeper number?

   Remember, if we leave a message for you, we *will only say*
   that we are calling from the Community Survey. Please let
   us know *if you prefer us not* to leave any message on an
   answering machine.

   1) **Daytime phone:** (_____) _____-_____ Best time to call: _____

   Who should we ask for? _____ Relationship: _____

Language:    1 = English    2 = Spanish    3 = Other

Note any special instructions: _____

_____

2) **Beeper:** (____) ____-_____ Best time to call: _____

Who should we ask for? _____ Relationship: _____

Language:    1 = English    2 = Spanish    3 = Other

Note any special instructions: _____

_____

3) **Evening phone:** (____) ____-_____ Best time to call: _____

Who should we ask for? _____ Relationship: _____

Language:    1 = English    2 = Spanish    3 = Other

Note any special instructions: _____

_____

9.  Are there relatives or friends who usually know how to reach you if you move?

Again, let me reassure you that we *will only say* we are calling from the Community Survey. Please let us know *if you prefer us not* to leave any message on an answering machine.

**(PROBES: Female relatives such as mother, sister, aunt)**

**(PROBES: Husband, lover, significant other, close friend, buddy)**

**Additional addresses can be listed in the space provided for interviewer comments.**

c/o Name: _____

Address/hangout:_____ Apt # _____

City: _____ State: _____ Zip code: _____

Phone: (____) ____-_____

Language:   1 = English   2 = Spanish   3 = Other

Best time to call: _____

Who should we ask for? _____

Relationship to respondent: _____

Note any special instructions: _____

_____

10. Are you currently going to a drug treatment program?

    1 = Yes     0 = No

    If yes:  Where: _____

    Address: _____

    What days? _____ What time? _____

11. Do you go to the Needle Exchange?     1 = Yes     0 = No

    If yes:  Where: _____

    Address: _____

    What days? _____ What time? _____

12. If you had nowhere to live, where would you go for food and shelter?

    Name: c/o _____

    Address:_____ Apt # _____

    City: _____ State: ____ Zip code: _____

    Phone: (____) ____-_____

    Language:   1 = English   2 = Spanish   3 = Other

    Best time to call: _____

Who should we ask for? _____

Relationship: _____

Note any special instructions: _____

_____

13. If we can't locate you at any of the above addresses, is there a local hangout where we could meet you?

    1 = Yes     0 = No

    Place _____

    Days _____ Time _____

    When the weather is bad, do you hang out somewhere different?

    1 = Yes     0 = No

    Place _____

    Days _____ Time _____

14. Where did you meet the outreach workers?

    Place _____

    Day _____ Time _____


**Interviewer comments or additional locating information/ addresses:**




_____

*Interviewer read:* Thank you very much for this information.

# INTERVIEWER OBSERVATIONS

1.  Gender:     1 = Male     2 = Female

2.  Ethnicity:     1 = Afr Amer     2 = Hisp     3 = Wh
    4 = As/Pac Is     5 = Am In/Al
    6 = Other (specify): _____

3.  Estimate of respondent's height: _____ feet _____ inches

4.  Estimate of respondent's weight _____ pounds

5.  Does the respondent wear glasses? 1 = Yes, 0 = No

6.  Eye color: _____

7.  Hair color: _____

    Hair length and style: _____

8.  Skin color/tone: _____

9.  Please note and describe any identifying marks, tattoos, or other unique physical characteristics of respondent. Try to supply enough information so that you can remember this person in 6 months (e.g., manner of speech, style of dress, personality traits):

    _____

    _____

    _____

    _____

# 4

# NOTES FROM THE FIELD: PROJECT PLANNING AND MANAGEMENT ISSUES

**STEPHANIE TORTU, PH.D., and THOMAS P. HAMILTON, with RAHUL HAMID, M.A.**

Whether directing a complex research project or overseeing the delivery of medical or social services, working with hard-to-reach populations requires careful advance planning. As noted by O. P. Kharbanda and Jeffrey Pinto, many management experts believe that inadequate planning is the primary cause of project failure. Although managers of field-based projects and community-based organizations (CBOs) may have been well trained as social science researchers, social workers, nurses, or public health educators, few have undergone formal training in management or learned such skills as how to evaluate job performance, set up communication systems, or address health and safety issues during their professional education.

Between us, we have not always known exactly what to do to ensure the success of our field-based projects, and sometimes we have had to improvise. Although among us we have had two decades of experience in directing complex research and service projects, we learned our project-planning strategies and management skills on the job, through a process of trial and error, often guided only by our intuition. As a result, we sometimes gingerly felt our way through territory that was new to us, such as designing communication systems or developing effective methods of performance evaluation, and we learned many lessons as we went along. We did not realize that time devoted to planning and preparing for a project was not "wasted" but would pay off in the long run. Over the years, we have had informal conversations with many colleagues involved in directing similar projects or running small community-based organizations. We discovered that few approached managing their first health intervention or directing their first research or social service project with confidence. Many issues came up that they had never had the opportunity to consider thoughtfully and thoroughly.

Research and service projects targeting hard-to-reach populations in difficult settings are especially challenging, and there are many obstacles to reaching goals. For example, people working on such projects often display a wide range of abilities, skills, and opinions regarding project goals. A large, grant-funded research project targeting homeless and runaway adolescents may employ both a doctoral-level data analyst and an outreach worker who did not complete high school, each of whom has different beliefs about the meaning and utility of research. The data analyst may be most interested in obtaining valid data, whereas the outreach worker may be most concerned with getting food for impoverished clients. The data analyst is probably convinced of the importance of empirical data, but the outreach worker may wonder why she has to fill out all those forms.

Projects conducted in difficult settings also have a high degree of background anxiety built into them by their very nature. Often, outreach and service delivery take place in risky inner-city environments. For example, we know several CBOs in New York City that deliver HIV prevention services in housing projects that are controlled by gangs, and our own staff has, on occasion, heard gunfire while in our storefront offices. In addition, given the nature of our work, many of the people receiving services or involved in our projects suffer from all the ills associated with urban poverty. Our staff is confronted on a daily basis with such problems as illiteracy, domestic violence, poor health, homelessness, drug addiction, HIV infection, unemployment, and depression. Working in this environment can be a source of anxiety for staff, and the feelings elicited can have a definite impact on the functioning of the research staff or the team of service providers.

Those who undertake the challenge of directing large research or service delivery projects need to prepare themselves adequately to achieve their goals. The major goal in directing a research project is to enable the research methodology to be implemented as planned and to ensure that the scientific integrity of the project is maintained. The major goal of service delivery is to enable services to reach those in need and to ensure that the services delivered are of the highest quality.

Who is this chapter written for? The information provided will be helpful primarily to a novice project manager, that is, someone who has been trained as a scientist, clinician, health educator, or other professional but has little experience directing research or service teams. This category includes senior management staff, such as principal investigators and project directors of research grants and executive directors of community-based organizations, all of whom have the bottom-line responsibility for field-based projects and all of whom must provide a work team with structure and guidance. It would also be useful for mid-level supervisors who report to senior management and will ultimately be responsible for implementing many of the procedures discussed. Finally, in keeping with the theme of this book, we are orienting this chapter to those who are working specifically with hard-to-reach or stigmatized populations in field settings outside mainstream institutions.

We became interested in sharing the guidelines we developed because we are convinced of their necessity. We have often observed that scientists planning research projects are understandably focused on research methodology and that clinicians are concerned first and foremost with the quality of care. As a result, many frequently overlook the issues we discuss here, to the detriment of both their staff and their clients.

## PREPARING THE WAY

### Field Site Safety and Health Are Basic

The management tasks on a large project do not begin the day the staff is hired and in place, but begin well before. One of the most important ways to prepare for staff is to make sure that the environment in which they are working is as safe and secure as possible. In institutions such as schools, hospitals, and health care centers, scientists and clinicians do not have to be concerned with safety and security. There are experienced staff to handle these concerns. However, in small or moderate-sized CBOs or on field-based, grant-funded projects, the responsibility for safety may be the province of the project director or the CBO's executive director. Two of us direct projects that are conducted in tough neighborhoods in New York City. We rent storefronts and old tenement flats where we conduct interviews, implement health-related interventions, and conduct medical testing. We have often spent months renovating sites to make them habitable, and one of our major concerns, which continues throughout the life of the project, is the issue of the security and safety of our staff. In our early experience, we had a number of break-ins and shootings, making the staff understandably nervous and jumpy. This anxiety was not connected with project tasks but rather with working in neighborhoods where violent crime was frequent. This taught us that one of the most important preparatory tasks was to make sure our working environment was as safe as possible, and we now know that a major aspect of project preparation is attention to the issues of safety and security. Before opening a field site for business, we ask the community affairs officer from the local police precinct to visit the field site and make suggestions regarding the security measures that should be taken. We also request a visit from a representative of the fire department. We have gotten advice from the police regarding how to secure windows, rooftops, and fire escapes, and we have had the fire department supervise the placement of our fire extinguishers and provide us with signs for fire exits. We have installed security cameras, gated windows, and buzzer systems in our storefronts, and we always hire a security guard–receptionist for opening and locking the sites, making sure that clients are not armed or openly carrying drugs or alcohol, and calming down the occasional recalcitrant client.

Sometimes, our security efforts have had unexpected consequences. In one particular instance, we were preparing to conduct a project that targeted drug users in East Harlem for an AIDS risk-reduction intervention. One of the neighborhood drug dealers was noticeably alarmed when we installed security cameras a few feet from a busy corner for dealing. Our security guard, who happened to live in the neighborhood and knew the dealer, approached him and explained the purpose of our project and why we installed cameras. He also invited the dealer into our field site to show the limited range of our cameras (the front door only) and, most importantly, let him know we were not undercover police! In neighborhoods like East Harlem, where a substantial part of life, both legal and illegal, takes place "on the streets," all movement is noted in the neighborhood intelligence system, and projects coming into a new area need to be alert to this fact.

Security measures are not limited to alarm systems and surveillance cameras. Once our projects begin, our field staff do not administer interviews, conduct medical testing, or lead health education groups unless the security guard is present on the site. We always make it known that there is no money on site: Project clients are paid for interviews with money orders that, thanks to a prior agreement we made, can be redeemed without identification at a nearby check-cashing establishment. Equipment such as computers, televisions, and VCRs are locked each evening in a closet. Whenever we conduct outreach on the streets of New York City, we always send people in teams, with cellular phones to use in emergencies. Generally, we know that if we feel relatively comfortable with the steps taken to ensure our staff's safety, this case will be communicated to our staff and go a long way toward allaying their anxiety.

In addition to making sure that our staff and field sites are relatively secure from thefts and break-ins, we have also become aware of other actions that may be needed to make the workplace safe and comfortable for staff. Many of our workers suffer from allergies and asthma, and it seems that the number of people suffering from these problems is on the rise. Thus, we have had to take steps to improve the air quality in many of the older buildings we use. Based on suggestions from medical personnel, we have installed dehumidifiers and air filtration systems, cleaned old heating ducts, and removed mold and mildew.

## Overseeing the Work Team

It is absolutely necessary to have someone on-site to oversee the staff, set priorities, and take responsibility for all aspects of field site operations on a daily basis. Given the realities of limited funding, senior management sometimes supposes that directing a field project can be done from the central office or as a part-time task. This is not so. On one of Stephanie's early research projects, a field coordinator was hired who was to oversee the operations of three field sites. His responsibilities included setting up interview and counseling schedules, administering the payment scheme to reimburse research subjects for interview time, and supervising a diverse field staff consisting of security guards, outreach workers, interviewers, and health educators. He was also responsible for ordering supplies, maintaining the physical site, arranging for repairs, and serving as a liaison between the senior managers and the field staff. This site coordinator worked in four locations: three field sites and also the central office of the organization. Senior management did not realize how much time and energy it would take to oversee the activities of three field sites. Not only was this a difficult, if not impossible, job, considering the variety of tasks that a good field coordinator must perform, but the need for the field coordinator to be in different places for a variety of activities frequently left the field sites without direct supervision, which had a disastrous effect on the project. In the absence of direct supervision, many relatively simple problems, such as plumbing difficulties or minor staff disputes, which could have been solved immediately if the field supervisor had been present, were often ignored until the point of crisis. Without a designated "responsible person" to step into a decision-making role, the field staff spent a great deal of time squabbling among themselves when a problem arose.

In particular, experience has taught us that adequate on-site supervision is especially important when behavioral problems are involved. For example, when a person routinely comes in late, does not handle clients in a tactful way, or continually makes mistakes with project accounts, these issues must be addressed immediately. Without routine on-site supervision, the behavior will not be addressed, and a seemingly small problem will ultimately affect the quality of everything that happens on that site. When staff members observe others getting away with unacceptable behavior because there is no on-site supervision, the result is bad morale and a growing resentment on the part of competent employees, who begin to take on the "if he can get away with it, I

*Field coordinators must be able to effectively supervise project staff both in storefronts and on streetside locations.*

can, too" attitude. It is virtually impossible to reverse this attitude once it takes hold, and it creates a lot of discontent.

Of course, field supervisors must be equipped with the skills needed to oversee all field site operations. These tasks include monitoring staff time and attendance, as well as mediating disagreements. In addition, supervisors should also be knowledgeable about such specialized topics as sexual harassment and grievance procedures and the administrative mechanisms used to deal with such issues. Finally, if the staff is unionized, site supervisors must be familiar with the details of the collective bargaining agreement. Before beginning a project and at periodic intervals during projects, we recommend that all staff with responsibility for direct supervision attend seminars, workshops, or training related to managing projects, especially those that feature case studies, role playing, and other methods that seek to teach through direct experience. Courses of this type can be useful in several ways: They can help people think systematically about the human issues they face on the job every day, assist with trouble shooting and problem solving, enhance knowledge, and teach new skills. In addition, they are also useful because they can enable groups of supervisors to realize they share common dilemmas and can learn from each other's experiences. However, do not have unrealistic expectations about what such workshops or training can do. They cannot make someone an effective supervisor instantly, and they cannot take people who are not suited to a supervisory position and magically provide them with the human traits and abilities needed to function. We like to think that such courses can take a diamond in the rough and polish it, but they cannot create a diamond from a lump of coal!

Although we may have convinced readers that a good site supervisor is a necessity, we must also warn that we have found it very difficult to fill this position. Ideally, the field coordinator should have supervisory experience, administrative ability, the capacity to carry out management's plans for structuring work groups, and the corresponding good judgment to react effectively to the unpredictable events that sometimes occur. The person should also have some knowledge of the substantive issues addressed by the project or organization. For example, much of our work concerns the health consequences of drug addiction. Therefore, in addition to having a knowledge of the commonly abused drugs in our city, we want our site supervisors to have basic information about AIDS, hepatitis, and tuberculosis. We also ask that our field supervisors have either knowledge of the neighborhood where we will be working or the ability to meet the members of the community directly involved with our client population, such as directors of drug treatment facilities and neighborhood health clinics.

By necessity, a field-based supervisor must be able to work independently and be well organized and attentive to details. It is also important that the field supervisor realize that he or she will probably have little contact with participants and will be mainly concerned with monitoring job performance and enabling the operations of field sites to take place. This is a job for a problem solver! It should be made clear in the initial interview that, if the little jobs do not get done, the field supervisor must be responsible enough to do them. Above all, however, hire someone with an innate respect for people and an ability to address the many human dilemmas that arise during a complex project. Although some qualities mentioned are discernible on a resume, these crucial ones are not.

Also, when interviewing job applicants, keep in mind that this situation is like a first date. The applicant is on his or her best behavior and trying hard to impress. However, having a good first date is no guarantee that the relationship will continue on such a good note. When interviewing prospective candidates, pay attention to intuition, but be sure to speak to those listed as references and check with former employers to confirm or refute that intuition. Make sure that the references know the applicant on a professional, work-related basis, not a personal one. An applicant who lists mainly personal references is warning you that something in his or her work history must remain hidden. In this litigious age, some people contacted for references will not give out damaging information about job applicants, but it may be possible to gauge how enthusiastic someone is by tone of voice or awkward pauses.

It helps the decision-making process to have as many colleagues as possible meet the candidates for site supervisor. And, because it is so rare that someone will go out of their way to warn *against* hiring a person, if someone known and trusted does this, take this warning very seriously. A colleague of ours was once issued such a warning, which he ignored, to his later regret. Another colleague hired someone who had a questionable job history with our own organization, and she neglected to check with previous project supervisors who could have told her that this applicant had serious problems in taking direction. When we have replaced field supervisors in the midst of a project, we have found it very helpful to introduce prospective candidates to the entire staff. We have also arranged to have the candidates for this position meet with the staff privately, without senior management present. Although the hiring decision remains with senior management, we have found the opinions of the staff to be valuable and right on the mark on many occasions.

A complex project is likely to employ people with a variety of skills, and usually the field supervisor will not have the expertise to oversee the performance of those with highly technical skills. For example, we employ experts in statistical analysis and data management, as well as phlebotomists, outreach workers, health educators, social workers, and interviewers. Thus, we have preferred to leave the evaluation and oversight of job performance to those who have the expertise that matches the skills being evaluated. Our site supervisors oversee the time and attendance of interviewers on research projects, but interviewing skills and data quality are overseen by staff trained in research methodology. Similarly, a community-based health project in the Bronx that provides acupuncture to its participants employs a nurse trained in Chinese medicine to supervise the practice of this technique. During the orientation phase of the project, which we discuss later, staff should have the opportunity to learn, in a very general way, about the variety of skills used on the project.

Once the preliminary health and safety procedures for the field site have been completed and a site supervisor has been hired, the next phases of the project require recruiting and hiring of project staff, preparing them for their work roles through training and orientation sessions, creating communication networks, and monitoring job performance.

Our assumption through much of the chapter is that a field-based research project will be time limited and that staff will move through the phases together. In other situations, such as a community-based organization, a mobile health clinic, or a drop-in center for adolescents, there is no time limitation because jobs are more or less permanent, and staff come and go at unpredictable times.

## RECRUITMENT

Interviewing top candidates for positions during the recruitment phase requires ruthless honesty about both the good and bad points of field-based projects. On time-limited and grant-funded research projects, people must realize that they are not interviewing for a job that will last indefinitely. People sometimes do not hear this when they are anxious for work. Also, clinicians or practitioners interviewed for a position on a research project must realize the degree of documentation that is necessary. Once a project starts, it always seems to come as a surprise to them. When interviewing someone for a position that involves technical expertise, such as data analyst, computer specialist, or nurse practitioner, make sure someone with a similar background participates in the interview and evaluates the job candidate. Make sure clinicians understand the difference between working in field-based settings and working in mainstream institutions.

During the hiring phase, consideration should be given to issues related to race, ethnicity, and other specific sociocultural factors that may be important to projects focused on hard-to-reach or hidden populations. As Bruce Stepherson indicated in his discussion of populations in need of health services (see Chapter 1), many people decline services from mainstream institutions because these people engage in illegal or stigmatized behaviors. Thus, staff who will conduct outreach, deliver services, or interview these hard-to-reach populations should be seen as approachable and unthreatening and be able to establish rapport quickly. It may be easier for hidden populations to trust those who are perceived as similar to themselves. Thus, when working with Puerto Ricans who speak Spanish or Haitian immigrants who speak Creole French, we always try to hire staff who either speak the language or have a similar ethnic background. Our projects targeting black women in New York City typically include black women from New York City on the team.

There are times when it may be desirable to match staff to project participants on qualities other than race or ethnicity. Such qualities may be broadly considered as "cultural factors." For example, when Michael Clatts and colleagues conducted the street-based research project for runaway adolescents described in Chapter 5, he hired youthful interviewers who, with their tattoos, body piercing, and street clothes, resembled the kids they were looking for. Prison-based studies often use ex-offenders as interviewers, and community-based organizations that distribute sterile needles to drug injectors sometimes prefer to hire former injectors. We do not want to give the impression that we use hard-and-fast rules to match staff and project participants on various dimensions; we do not do this unless there is a scientific reason to do so on our research projects. Nor do we hire people based on these qualities alone. Our first criterion is that a person has the qualifications to do the job. However, consideration of cultural factors is a part of our decision-making process because it is relevant to our work, and anyone working with hard-to-reach or hidden populations should consider whether it is relevant to theirs. For example, hiring ex-offenders to interview those incarcerated in prisons not only makes it possible for interviewers to gain rapport quickly but also can be useful in other ways. When, for example, based on his knowledge of prison life, an interviewer spots responses that may be invalid, his insight improves the quality of the data on a research project. In another instance, former drug users can be of assistance in designing health-related materials for drug users because they are familiar with street slang, and this knowledge can make the health information more accessible to the population being targeted. Women who have been on welfare and are working on a project aimed at getting welfare recipients into the workforce can be powerful when they are trained as team leaders and counselors. In all these cases, the experiential wisdom gained by being in prison, in the drug life, or on welfare can be an asset to a project. Sometimes this experiential wisdom is combined with a keen intellect and engaging personality, and the contributions such a person can make are invaluable. In Chapter 6, our colleague Bea Krauss discusses this issue in greater detail.

If the nature of a project makes it necessary or desirable to consider hiring someone with a nontraditional employment background, several things enter into the decision. For example, we hire many people with histories of drug and alcohol addiction, some of whom have had minimal experience with paid employment but are very skilled in making it on the streets of New York City or hustling for money by filling roles in the underground economy. (At this time of changing welfare regulations, many such people will be trying to enter the workforce.) We hire people with nontraditional backgrounds partly for their street savvy, but certain of these habits do not transfer well to a research site or community-based organization. Applicants must know what is appropriate behavior in each setting. Often, the basics, such as demeanor and dress, are observable during the job interview, and it is certainly appropriate to discuss the issues of workplace socialization with any person listed as a reference. Do not assume anything! It is a real advantage if applicants have had some experience at a "regular job" or in a volunteer position where they have learned such things as how to report on time and how to accept supervision and work within a given structure, but this is not often the case.

Sometimes, people who have not had traditional types of paid employment may require socialization into the workplace culture and an understanding of the norms governing behavior in the work environment. This includes introducing people to such things as on-the-job dress codes, the importance of being on time and notifying supervisors when sick, and the necessity to take direction from a supervisor and complete assigned tasks. These habits of the workplace are something most of us take for granted, but we have learned this is not the case with those whose experience with paid employment, or even volunteer work, has been minimal or nonexistent. For example, Stephanie once learned that someone on her research team had taken his shoes off in the reception area of the field site and begun clipping his toenails! She responded to this faux pas and other instances of inappropriate behavior by developing a code of behavioral standards for the work setting, which we have included in Figure 4-1. During the training and orientation phase of the project, we review these standards and make our expectations clear to the staff. Education regarding workplace behavioral norms can also be formal, such as in job training programs. Some of it can be accomplished in the orienta- tion phase and through individualized supervision sessions, and some of it can be learned on the job by observing more experi- enced staff. Depending on the type of project, all of these methods may be used.

We have mentioned several times the importance of checking references, but people with limited employment experience, such as women on welfare or ex–drug users who may not have worked

**FIGURE  4-1    Field Site Guidelines: An Example from a
New York City–Based Project**

---

*Guidelines*

*Reminder:* A person's dignity is recognized when we act with respect toward that person. This is the foundation for all the guidelines that follow.

1. The waiting room at the site is part of our health intervention with project participants. A tone of professionalism and the modeling of appropriate behavior are expected.

   • Personal conversations and issues should be discussed in private, not in the waiting room or any other public area.

   • Staff should not do paperwork in the waiting room unless it is per- tinent to the project; work-related duties that do not involve con-

**FIGURE 4-1** *Continued*

tact with project participants should be performed in staff offices. All confidential information should remain in the appropriate offices, with procedures in place to protect the confidentiality of the information.

2. Coffee and refreshments purchased with grant-related funds are for project participants only. Unfortunately, we are unable to use grant-related funds to purchase food for staff.

3. Neither interviews nor groups should be interrupted by anyone for any reason except a serious emergency. Phone calls, messages, and the need for paperwork are not serious emergencies.

4. No visitors of any kind may appear on site unless prior authorization by assistant project directors or coordinators has been made. This refers to friends, relatives, former staff members, and others. Both confidentiality and security are threatened by strangers on the site.

5. Before entering another staff member's office, make sure there are no project participants with the staff member. Then ask for permission to enter. Whenever possible, use your own office for work and phone calls; respect the space and privacy of other workers.

6. Please talk or play radios in modulated tones. Most offices are not fully soundproof; conversations and radios can be heard by others and may disturb them.

7. Contact with project participants beyond your job description is inappropriate and may affect research and intervention outcomes. Staff must keep boundaries between their professional and personal lives.

8. Serious ethical violations include the breaching of confidentiality and close social contacts with project participants outside the bounds of either research or service. These ethical violations are most serious and, if you are aware of any such violation, you should discuss this confidentially with any senior staff person (assistant project director, project director, or principal investigator).

for many years because of their addiction, sometimes provide references that are not connected with paid employment. For example, we have had employees who have listed supervisors of volunteer services and directors of job training internships as references. Such references should be taken as seriously as those for paid employment, especially if the skills used during these experiences are relevant. In many instances, volunteer and internship experiences may have also taught the applicant the important social skills needed to function in a work environment.

## TRAINING AND ORIENTATION

During the training and orientation phase, attention must be paid to two parallel but complementary domains. First, staff should be trained to do the specific tasks in their job descriptions. This is the time when individuals learn how they are supposed to code data, provide health education or demonstrate health-related skills, or make social service referrals. Second, this phase is also the time when people begin to learn to work effectively as a group and are socialized regarding work-related norms. We feel that this is a critical time in the life of any project, and careful attention to the orientation phase pays off in the long run. When beginning projects with 10 to 20 staff members, most of our orientation activities are conducted in a group setting, and the guidelines we offer here reflect that. Nonetheless, much of what we discuss in this section can be accomplished on an individual level as well.

During our orientation phase, staff are given a welcoming packet that includes an employee handbook. All organizations should have a publication of this type in which personnel policies, benefits, grievance procedures, and related issues are described. Project-related materials, consisting of a training and orientation agenda as well as organizational charts outlining relationships between project staff and describing project roles, are also distributed. We carefully review and discuss the project management structure so that there is no confusion about performance oversight, and we explain the mechanisms that we will put in place to evaluate job performance. We also describe the substantive aspects of the project, whether it is concerned with conducting research, providing services, or a combination of both. When projects are concerned with both research and service, we stress the interdependence of both aspects to head off any research-versus-service antagonism. When conducting orientation for research projects, we work hard to make the idea of research less mystifying for the non-research staff. For example, we present and discuss the research design and explain such things as threats to validity, the necessity of documentation, and the importance of a consistent approach to participants in research projects. We feel that it is important for people to understand why they are asked to do things that would not have been expected of them in a nonresearch setting.

Also included in our orientation and training is a discussion of the ethical standards of scientific research with human subjects, especially the importance of confidentiality. In preparation for research projects, we discuss the institutional review board and its role in the project and describe the certificate of confidentiality we typically receive from the Department of Health and Human Services. (This protects data on federally funded research grants from subpoena.) We also outline plans for how to transport research and/or medical data from the field site to the central office without jeopardizing client confidentiality. These issues are important for any projects or organizations that routinely collect medical or sensitive information that must be protected. Chapter 7 discusses confidentiality and other ethical issues in more detail.

Depending on the project, our training sessions sometimes last for three to four days. During our first projects, we discovered that staff love to get training certificates after this experience. Therefore, when the training sessions have been completed, we present certificates to the staff as part of a "closing ceremony." They are greatly prized by our nonprofessional staff and serve as a genuine morale booster. One other accoutrement our staff greatly desire is their own set of business cards, which we also provide at the end of the training sessions.

## COMMUNICATION AND
## PERFORMANCE EVALUATION

The major management task during the maintenance phase is to implement a project-based communication network that ensures the flow of project-related information, provides for the oversight of day-to-day job performance, helps keep people on track and accountable, and enables problem areas to be identified and addressed. In this section, we describe several strategies we have used:

- Informal, performance-oriented, "on-the-job" discussions
- Individual, formal supervision sessions
- Morning briefings
- General staff meetings

### Informal Field Discussions

These are work-oriented, informal discussions that naturally develop in the field between a supervisor and a staff member in the course of the workday. We have found that this is an excellent opportunity for a supervisor to observe job performance, ask questions, and learn in a more direct way about the day-to-day routine of the employee. This type of interaction can be less intimidating than more formal meetings, and staff sometimes use this opportunity to broach issues they may not have been comfortable addressing in individual supervision sessions or regular staff meetings. Often, the very informality of the interaction provides the supervisor with important insights about a person's judgment and work performance that could not be gained in other settings. Informal field discussions also enable the supervisor to address certain issues firsthand, diminishing the potential for staff to receive misinformation about work-related issues from second- and third-party sources.

**An On-the-Job Discussion**

On one of Tom's projects, a supervisor on a street-based health intervention project, Ms S, observed a newly hired female outreach worker, Ms Z, over a period of days and noticed that the woman was very enthusiastic when she engaged female clients but reacted apprehensively when she engaged or approached male clients. When Ms S mentioned this, Ms Z became defensive and denied that she acted in the observed manner. Ms S calmly recounted several occasions that she had noted over the course of 3 days and then explained that many workers, including herself, have biases relating to such characteristics as gender, race, religion, and sexual preference. She explained that this was a normal human reaction, but it was necessary for Ms Z to think about her biases and work through them to do her job more effectively. In response, Ms Z admitted that men had abused her in the past and that she preferred not to interact with them. The supervisor made a mental note of her difficulty and began to formulate ideas and strategies that could help Ms Z with her dilemma. The supervisor reviewed the available options with Ms Z, including a possible referral to the organization's employee assistance counseling program or attendance at support groups. This issue may never have been raised if the behavior had not been observed firsthand, and it was unlikely to have come out in a formal staff meeting. Over time, with assistance from counseling, Ms Z was able to resolve the problem enough so that it no longer interfered with her work.

## Individual Supervision Sessions

Individual supervision sessions are structured, formal meetings. In this forum, a supervisor can address both positive and negative aspects of performance, note specific examples of success, and recommend corrective actions, if necessary. In some instances, this may also be the time to discuss job-related plans for the future, such as further training or achieving certain work-related goals (e.g., learning new skills, completing high school, finishing a college degree). We recommend that formal supervision occurs at least once every 6 months, and a record kept of these sessions is very helpful. We also feel that it is important for staff to come to these meetings with some items of their own for discussion, and we encourage a collaborative style of conversation between the supervisor and the staff member. Topics for this session include an individual's major job-related accomplishments since the last formal meeting, projected future goals, and the outline of a plan to achieve these goals. Other issues that often come up for discussion include setting priorities and time management; performance deficits or minor behavioral problems can also be addressed, but, as we illustrate later, these should not be the sole focus of the meeting. Plans to correct the deficit should be discussed and agreed on by both parties. A good supervisor will welcome this dynamic interaction because, if done correctly, individual supervision should leave no doubt about the organization's or project's expectations regarding job performance and development. (Stephanie has tried to use this session to get feedback from staff about her own performance as project director. However, staff have been understandably reticent about addressing this issue, and we have found this is not the forum to use for collecting this information.) For the novice supervisor, we have found that the initial tendency during these meetings is to focus only on performance deficits.

Next, we have listed some of the action guidelines we use in conducting individual supervision sessions:

**1.** Begin the session by reviewing positive aspects of the person's job performance, and identify any skill-based areas where change may be needed. Design an improvement plan with the employee by specifying corrective measures. The plan should use behavioral terms to specify the changes needed. In other words, do not state, "I will improve my interviewing skills" but "I will learn to recognize skip patterns and increase my accuracy with responses that have numerical categories."

## The Hammer

For about the first two years in his role as field site supervisor and manager, Mr T used individual supervision sessions in one way: to address negative performance issues or disciplinary problems. His use of this tool earned him the nickname The Hammer, a nickname based directly on how Mr T interacted during individual supervision sessions. At the mere mention of someone's supervision session, staff could be overheard saying to the person about to enter Mr T's office, "Oh, I hope you're prepared to get hammered for whatever you've done wrong." The Hammer meant that he was a *hard-hitting* and *no-nonsense* supervisor who, for the most part, was interested only in criticizing and driving workers to perform better with little or no concern for anything else. Although Mr T's style intimidated many of them, it did bring noticeable and beneficial results in the short term. As time went on, however, both senior managament and Mr T noticed that his style served only to create a group of people who functioned primarily out of fear, not respect. Moreover, folks were afraid to share their ideas and suggestions or mention their goals for the future because the opportunity was never present in Mr T's supervision discussions. Mr T's misuse of individual supervisory sessions had fostered an environment in which staff felt intimidated, fearful, and at times useless, causing many to function ineffectively and thus jeopardizing the success of the program. Mr T's supervision sessions were solely negative experiences and became the breeding grounds for poor morale among the project staff. Senior management recognized the problem and began working with Mr T to change his approach to supervisory sessions.

2. Describe the means to improve performance; for example, this may involve further training, more practice doing a task, or working with and closely observing a more experienced employee.

**3.** Review progress in improving job-related skills or time and attendance problems by providing regular (at least weekly) feedback through informal interaction; reward success with praise! When in the process of changing behavior, people need frequent reinforcement to enhance learning new skills.

**4.** Encourage the person to set definite time limits for both immediate ("in the next year") and long-term goals ("in five years"). An example of an immediate goal would be "In one year, I will learn to perform phlebotomy in order to upgrade my position on this project." A long-term goal could be "In five years, I want to have completed my public health degree and begin work as a public health educator."

**5.** For both long- and short-term goals, people should describe at least one action, stated in behavioral terms, that they will take toward achieving their goal; for example, "I will register for the phlebotomy training in the next month," and "I will take one course next semester toward a public health degree."

**6.** Review progress toward long- and short-term goals in the next formal supervision session, and be sure to reward progress appropriately. Suitable and cost-free rewards for reaching milestones are praise, certificates of achievement, promotions, and special mention at staff meetings.

## Morning Briefings

Morning briefings are daily meetings for all staff held at the beginning of the day for approximately 15 to 20 minutes. They are most appropriate when people function as teams and perform their jobs in settings that are subject to rapidly changing conditions. In our own experience, morning briefings promote team building and are beneficial to street-based outreach projects, including mobile medical vans. Projects of this sort can be affected by such circumstances as extreme weather conditions and construction projects, breakdowns in public transportation, street-based police actions, and radical changes in welfare and health care regulations. Morning briefings are very similar to the roll call meetings that most law enforcement agencies utilize at the start of a shift. Fundamentally, the objectives for morning briefings are to assemble staff, delegate work assignments, ensure that street-based and office-based activities are coordinated when necessary, and briefly discuss any issues that may affect street-based work. This is also an opportunity for staff to mention any concerns they may have about the upcoming workday and share information with the project that may affect the workday. This process can be a vital ingredient in team building because it fosters collaboration among staff to develop effective strategies to counter changes in street dynamics.

## Staff Meetings

Regular meetings for all project staff are important for the purposes of routine project-wide communication and team-based problem solving. Senior management, such as executive directors, principal investigators, and project directors, should structure the activities during these meetings. We have generally found it useful to meet at least twice a month, but at times it is necessary to meet more often. For example, we meet weekly in the early stages of a project to closely monitor activity to determine if procedures are being implemented as planned, and we also meet weekly after introducing a major change in protocol. We distribute meeting agendas, and sometimes we serve refreshments and use this time to celebrate individual or project-wide milestones. As part of every staff meeting, progress reports are given by the relevant staff. For example, on research projects, reports are provided on the number of subjects recruited or interviews completed, and on service projects, reports are given on the number of clients served and the specific services received.

General staff meetings can also be used for educational purposes. For example, we have often invited speakers to address topics of concern to our staff, and we provide regular updates on public health issues that may be relevant for both the population we serve and our own staff. For example, in the early 1990s, a number of people became concerned about tuberculosis because of a newspaper article on the rise of a drug-resistant strain of the disease among drug users. Staff were alarmed by the news, and project management needed expert advice in this area. Thus, we invited representatives from the Department of Health and used the staff meeting as an opportunity to question these health experts. This was very successful in allaying anxiety and also demonstrated that senior management recognized and reacted quickly to the concerns of the staff.

At times, we also feature presentations about our own project during staff meetings. As project data are analyzed and reports prepared for conferences, this information is presented to everyone and often results in lively discussions! We consider this type of reporting to be an important way to enable staff to see the results of their labor in an immediate and tangible form. We have also benefited from reviewing results with our staff because there have been many times when their reactions and comments have helped us in interpreting our data. Once, when resources permitted, we published our own project newsletter, featuring the personal and professional accomplishments of the staff. These were distributed at staff meetings, and people always enjoyed seeing their names in print. In addition to providing a means of project-wide communication, this visibly improved morale.

## Other Issues: Down Time, Work Role Confusion, and Turnover

Occasionally, field-based projects and community-based organizations must address the issue of down time. For example, street-based projects may experience lulls in activity during the extreme heat of summer and cold of winter, when clients often remain indoors. Not doing anything for hours at a time is demoralizing for staff, and, with idle time, the scope of minor problems and simple inconveniences is magnified; small difficulties begin to appear insurmountable, and staff members begin to complain. One of the ways to minimize idleness is to train people to perform tasks that can be done when there is a lull in their assigned duties. For example, our interviewers sometimes conduct outreach or "clean" or code data when people do not show up for interviews. We have also encouraged health educators, social workers, and counselors to write papers for professional journals during their down time or catch up on their paperwork and formal reports.

During some projects, it has also been necessary to confront work role confusion and misunderstandings concerning job duties. For example, we once noticed that interviewers would sometimes get involved in counseling clients, and social workers would offer medical advice. This type of behavior usually arises out of a sincere desire to do more to help the client, and we have noted that this problem must be addressed on both research and service projects. On research projects, there are usually scientific reasons for the strict delineation of roles. On service projects, staff are often upset when they perceive that someone is encroaching on their specific roles. The only antidote to role confusion is to be on the alert for it during supervision sessions, and, when it happens, review job descriptions and monitor performance carefully until the behavior stops.

Most projects are faced with turnover at some point, especially among employees in the lower-paid positions. Integrating new staff into an existing group can be difficult, and both senior management and field supervisors need to devote the time necessary to provide a proper orientation to the project or organization. We have devised a welcoming packet for all new staff that includes the written materials distributed at the original orientation and the names of project staff who have volunteered to answer their questions and help them become integrated into the work team.

## Behavioral Issues

Many of the best human qualities come out in the workplace, but so do some of the worst. People can be cooperative, empathetic, hardworking, and kind to others, but we have also seen people squabble, gossip, complain incessantly, and treat each other with a distinct lack of respect. We believe that the management guidelines described in this chapter can help keep behavioral problems at a minimum. When the work environment is structured to foster regular communication and staff are respected by their supervisors and given the training and resources needed to succeed at their jobs, the result is good morale and fewer behavioral problems. Nevertheless, there will be times on every project, or within every CBO, when staff behavior requires managers' attention.

Unfortunately, on some occasions the behavioral problems on our projects were so serious that we had to dismiss employees. Serious offenses, for which dismissal is the only correct action, include committing an act of violence in the workplace, stealing money or equipment, or being drunk or high during work. Before dismissing an employee, it is wise to enlist the assistance of your human resources department, and keep in mind that legal counsel may be necessary. Organizations that sponsor grant-funded research and small community-based agencies will have legal counsel available for use in situations such as these. Other issues that may require legal guidance include charges by employees of discrimination, sexual harassment, or violations of human rights, either by other employees or by the organization itself. It is beyond the scope of this chapter to treat these issues in detail. In our experience of dealing with these types of serious offenses, it is important to be familiar with the organization's administrative policies and personnel procedures and carefully document the relevant events and conversations.

Most of the behavioral problems confronted on research and service projects are less serious. However, behavioral issues such as conflict between employees that seriously impairs job performance have a definite impact on the morale of everyone working on the project, and it is important to address them quickly. We cannot anticipate all of the particular difficulties a project will face, but we have come up with some points to consider in trying to resolve problems.

## Mediating a Language Gap

We employ many people who are fluent in both English and Spanish, and we have faced serious problems connected to the use of language in the workplace. On one of our street-based projects, those who did not understand Spanish became offended and reported vague feelings of paranoia after being present at a few Spanish conversations that ended with laughter and giggling. Those who were linguistically excluded believed they were being mocked, and they confronted the Spanish speakers and told them angrily to speak in English. The Spanish speakers could not understand the problem, and, further, they did not think their freedom to speak Spanish in the workplace should be curtailed. As project directors, we were forced to step in and resolve this issue before it did irreparable harm to morale. Over the course of a few days, we met with both groups, listened to various points of view, and made sure that the Spanish speakers were not actually insulting anyone. To resolve this conflict and ensure that this problem did not recur, we emphasized the importance of common courtesy. In bilingual situations, it is polite to go out of your way not to exclude anyone; we advised the Spanish speakers to translate or ask permission to speak Spanish. In general, these measures worked to reassure our monolingual staff that nothing insulting was being said and that Spanish was not being used to exclude them.

We have several action guidelines to consider:

**1.** Behavioral problems that seriously impede the ability of folks to do their jobs should be addressed by management. Minor human failings (such as grouchiness or mild antipathy between co-workers) may not affect project goals directly, however, and people generally find ways of coping without management intervention.

**2.** Employees do not have to love each other. Mutual respect and tolerance—in order to get the job done—is acceptable! It is management's job to communicate this and, more important, to model this approach for staff.

**3.** If a behavioral problem directly affects the goals of the project or the organization, it should be dealt with immediately; otherwise, it will escalate and become more serious.

**4.** In negotiating a dispute between two employees, listening carefully is more important than laying down the law. At first, listen to each disputant separately. After hearing both sides, mediate a discussion in which mutually acceptable solutions are sought. This process should take place in several steps over the course of a few days to allow time for reflection.

**5.** Do not try to reason with anyone who is angry. Give him or her time to calm down, and do not respond in kind. The manager's job is to stay cool. Lost tempers lead to escalation and get in the way of problem solving.

**6.** Sometimes conflict is healthy because its resolution may lead to improved morale.

## Ending a Project

On time-limited projects such as research grants, the end of the project must always be kept in mind. In health and social service organizations, the vagaries of funding, changing policies, and shifts in community-based service needs often lead to phasing out whole sites and work teams. In these situations, project directors need to ensure that the termination process is carried out in a systematic manner. The end of a project is fraught with mixed emotions. Although staff are proud of their accomplishments, many have to face the instability of unemployment and the need to look for a new job. To ease these feelings, we suggest using individual supervision sessions to discuss promotion, other job possibilities, and, if possible, opportunities for further schooling or training. Assure valued staff that they will be kept in mind for future projects, and, when appropriate, offer to write recommendations or serve as a reference.

Closing a project also presents many operational concerns. Project records need to be finalized, final evaluation reports need to be completed, and the movement of supplies and furniture has to be orchestrated. Finally, financial documents and records must be prepared for auditing, and a final financial report must be generated. The manager has to choose the staff needed to complete these tasks and set up a time table for completion.

## CONCLUSION

This chapter is not intended to be a primer on management. For that, we refer readers to the work of Peter Drucker (see the recommended readings) or other theorists of management. Nor is this chapter about leadership. Rather, based on our own experience, we hope that we have pointed out some of the issues, many unforeseen, that may arise in large projects targeted at hard-to-reach populations. We also described some of the strategies we have used to deal with these challenges. Finally, we reviewed the major management tasks associated with each phase of a project and provided the guidelines we use for all phases of research and service projects. We do not offer these guidelines as a fixed formula for managing complex projects, nor are they meant to be the final word on directing a staff that works with hard-to-reach populations. Rather, our guidelines are meant to stimulate thinking about the complexities involved in the day-to-day running of such projects and to underline the necessity of thinking through many of the issues covered here before hiring staff and implementing the project. Over time, we have noticed that the management strategies we describe have helped us to create a work environment that fosters success. The major factors that have ensured the relatively smooth running of our projects have been that individual and team goals are clearly defined, the means to achieve them are provided, and communication networks fit the needs of the project.

## SUGGESTED READINGS

Dreger, J. B. (1992). *Project management: Effective scheduling.* New York: Van Nostrand Reinhold.

Drucker, P. F. (1985). *Management: Tasks, responsibilities, practices.* New York: First Harper Colophon.

Drucker, P. F. (1990). *Managing the nonprofit organization: Principles and practices.* New York: HarperCollins.

Frame, J. D. (1994). *The new project management.* San Francisco: Jossey-Bass.

Gilbreath, R. D. (1986). *Winning at project management: What works, what fails and why.* New York: Wiley.

Kharbanda, O. P., & Pinto, J. K. (1996). *What made Gertie gallop: Learning from project failures.* New York: Van Nostrand Reinhold.

Overton, G. W. (Ed.). *Guidebook for directors of nonprofit corporations.* Chicago: American Bar Association.

# 5

# USING A SYSTEMS PERSPECTIVE AND COMPUTER TECHNOLOGY IN PREVENTION RESEARCH

**MICHAEL C. CLATTS, PH.D., W. R. DAVIS, PH.D., MARIE BRESNAHAN, M.P.H., and HELENE LAUFFER, M.P.A.**

Available data indicate there are about 2 million homeless adolescents in the United States, and it has been estimated that as many as 200,000 live as permanent residents of the streets. This population is composed of a complex mix of young people who have different reasons for being on the streets and varying abilities to manage street life. Although some have left home of their own volition, others have been forced out, and some are from already homeless or fragmented families. Whatever the size and distribution of this population, and regardless of the antecedents of adolescent homelessness, we know that the lives of these youth are characterized by poor nutrition, chronic exhaustion, and repeated exposure to violence and victimization. Homeless adolescents are vulnerable to exposure to the elements and a wide variety of health problems, including high rates of upper respiratory ailments, untreated tuberculosis, exposure to sexually transmitted diseases, unplanned pregnancies, and chronic drug dependency. In

125

recent years, the prevalence of HIV infection and AIDS in this population has also increased dramatically.

In New York City, the development of outreach and health-related prevention services targeted specifically to street youth began in the mid-1980s. At that time, relatively little was known about these youth, but their numbers appeared to be increasing. There were also indications that they were at very high risk for becoming involved in the use of illicit drugs as well as the sex economies of the Times Square area and West Greenwich Village. Most were assumed to be runaways from outside the New York City metropolitan area and in need of crisis intervention services. Street outreach was used as a strategy for reaching youth in need and linking them up with the mainstream social service system. When outreach workers began to work with youth on the streets, they discovered that the population was quite different from what was originally expected. Most were from the New York City area, rather than from other parts of the country. Many did not have families to which they could return or came from family environments that were hazardous to their physical and emotional well-being.

At the time, the mainstream New York City service delivery system was ill equipped to meet the special needs of this particular population. For example, access to drug treatment was very limited, and there were virtually no services for gay and lesbian youth. In addition, the mainstream service delivery system was not prepared to establish the special types of service-oriented relationships required by homeless youth. Many of these youth had already been exposed to profound emotional or physical trauma before ever arriving on the streets, and these experiences were exacerbated by the violence and exploitation that is part and parcel of the harsh street life in New York City. As a result, mainstream adolescent services were often unprepared to meet the complex social, economic, and emotional needs they presented. When street youth did gain access to mainstream New York City service settings, outreach staff noted that they were unable to function at the pace such programs required, often leading to disastrous outcomes. For example, rather than obtaining medical care at the large, impersonal medical institutions that were often the only source of aid available to them, many young people delayed seeking care until their health conditions became critical.

As a result of working among these youth and developing a deeper understanding of their needs and capacities, outreach staff from several New York City programs found it necessary to develop on-site service delivery programs tailored to attract, rather than alienate or intimidate, street youth. Although initially very limited in scope, these services were highly individualized. Street outreach continued as a key service delivery approach but was also increasingly used as a method for drawing youth to drop-in centers, where more comprehensive services were provided and where service relationships established on the streets could be further developed. Services provided at these drop-in centers included responding to the daily needs for food, clothing, and showers, alongside an array of counseling, educational, and health services. These newly developed service centers were distinct from traditional or mainstream service venues in three major ways. First, they were designed to afford youth as much flexibility as possible in utilizing the various service components; second, they focused on addressing needs identified by the youth themselves; and third, they worked with clients at a pace determined in large part by the youth themselves. As these centers were being developed in the mid-1980s, medical and social service agencies in New York City were at the same time struggling to cope with the challenges of the AIDS epidemic. Homeless youth, many of whom were drug users and also involved in street-based survival sex work, were among those at highest risk for HIV infection and AIDS.

In 1991, the Centers for Disease Control and Prevention (CDC) funded a cooperative agreement in eight sites across the United States. The purpose of this project was to evaluate the impact of outreach services on reducing the risk of HIV infection among vulnerable populations. In this chapter, we describe the Youth at Risk (YAR) project, one of the eight programs that received CDC funding to evaluate street outreach services to homeless youth. Over the course of five years, we worked with all of the outreach programs that provide services in the central Manhattan area, including Midtown (Times Square), the West Village, and the East Village, locations with high concentrations of homeless youth. In this chapter, we describe the use of a *systems* model as an approach to community organization and HIV prevention services. We offer this case as an example that we hope will stimulate other community-based organizations to pool resources and work cooperatively to enhance the capacity and performance of the prevention services delivery system in their communities.

## CONCEPTUAL UNDERPINNINGS: A SYSTEMS MODEL

Over the course of the last decade, a number of competing behavioral change models have been developed in an attempt to forge a coherent public health approach to change behaviors implicated in the spread of HIV infection. The scope of this chapter does not permit a detailed discussion of the complex theoretical issues that attend the development of models, such as Prochaska's Stages of Change Theory, Janz and Becker's Health Belief Model, and Fishbein and colleagues' Theory of Reasoned Action, many of which underpin publicly funded AIDS prevention efforts. It is sufficient to note here that these models have been primarily concerned with enhancing an individual's perception and skills needed to engage in HIV-related risk reduction.

Certainly, factors such as knowledge, belief, and intention, as well as skill building, are important considerations in reducing the risk of HIV infection. One of the limitations of these cognitive approaches, however, is that they often hold the external environment and the interpersonal circumstances in which an individual lives as constant in relation to the everyday behavioral choices that individuals can actually exercise. They also implicitly assume that individual decision making in relation to risk is not significantly encumbered by these external factors. Unfortunately, these assumptions are not always true in the case of street youth, and we found that the relevance and utility of these models were quite limited for the purposes of intervening in the kinds of circumstances that confront many street youth. Generally speaking, street youth are very knowledgeable about how HIV is transmitted and how to reduce their own risk for exposure. Street youth are also highly motivated to avoid HIV risk. The economic circumstances in which these youth live, however, often serve to limit their ability to protect themselves against HIV, and, indeed, it is precisely their dependence on the street economy that makes these youth so vulnerable to the risks inherent in street life. The existing service delivery system is poorly equipped, both in scope and in form, to provide substantive alternatives to the street economy, and as a result many youth are unable to find the means to leave street life.

Because of substantial gaps in the existing prevention services delivery system that became evident in the initial phases of the study, we employed a "systems perspective" to develop our intervention model, a model that was largely directed at enhancing the service delivery environment to which youth were exposed. The term *systems* derives from a body of research in human ecology that examines the interaction and interdependence between host and environment. In the context of HIV prevention, environment includes the physical environment in which risk behavior occurs, the interpersonal relationships through which risk is transacted, and the larger economic and political conditions in which these relationships are embedded. It also includes the service delivery system itself, the level of resources available, the way in which resources and services are distributed, and the manner in which they are delivered. (This is explained in greater detail in the 1995 NIDA monograph listed in the suggested readings at the end of this chapter.)

## SUMMARY OF RESEARCH FINDINGS

The study was organized into three components: (1) an initial community assessment process (CAP), (2) a formal street-based survey of youth involvement in risk behavior and exposure to prevention services, and (3) the development and implementation of multiple enhancements of existing prevention services. The first phase included a qualitative assessment of existing outreach services, using information derived from semistructured interviews with three sources: administrators of service agencies working with youth on the streets, outreach workers and others who interacted directly with the youth, and homeless youth themselves, whom we contacted on the streets. The second component of the study involved the administration of a formal empirical survey of street youth, including details of their involvement in drug and sexual risk and their exposure to and utilization of prevention-related services (e.g., street outreach, needle exchange programs, health services, drug treatment, and emergency housing). Information from the first two components was used to plan the third component, developing and implementing strategically designed enhancements of existing intervention services.

## The Community Assessment Process

The purpose of the CAP was to describe the existing services available to street youth and to identify ways in which the behavioral impact of existing services could be enhanced. We felt that it was important to gain information from a variety of perspectives. Thus, YAR staff had discussions with program administrators and policy makers, as well as a broad range of direct service providers, including drop-in center counselors and street outreach staff. We also conducted similar interviews with youth themselves regarding outreach services they had received or wished to receive. We found that the discussions were invaluable in helping us understand the background and history of the existing service delivery system and how these services were distributed in the community.

Service providers' descriptions of what they felt the youth needed, as well as what they themselves felt they needed in doing their jobs, centered around problems of inadequate resources and difficulty in maintaining coherence in service delivery relationships. Providers described having to, in effect, ration services, limiting the kinds and amount of services available to a given youth so as not to have to turn away another youth. Many described concerns about the special needs of particular segments of the population, such as gay and lesbian youth. Issues regarding sexuality and drug abuse were noted to be major barriers to service delivery. Problems in accessing health care were also reported. Service providers revealed being overwhelmed by the scope and complexity of the needs of the youth and frustrated by the scarcity of material and programmatic resources available. Many service providers also described feeling that they did not have the specific skills needed to care for these youth, particularly in relation to the complex issues surrounding HIV. Case management staff pointed to a wide variety of problems in attempting to secure mainstream services for street youth, including difficulties in communication with other programs and New York City's large, complex, and generally inefficient social services system. Many of the frontline providers described the substantial emotional burden of working with this population, especially the enormous feeling of loss associated with youth who had died from violence, suicide, and AIDS. Many reported feeling burned out and unsure of how long they would be able to continue doing this kind of work. Providers, particularly program administrators, also described frustration about the complex patchwork of sources of funding for services, the instability of available funding, and the heavy burden of widely divergent application and reporting requirements.

In addition to qualitative interviews with service providers, we also conducted a series of consumer-oriented interviews with youth themselves. An analysis of the data from these interviews was conducted to understand the personal experiences of youth in obtaining services and their perceptions of what worked well and what was needed. The 51 youth who were interviewed ranged in age from 13 through 23 and reflected different degrees of involvement in street life, as well as different lengths of time on the street. The majority of contacts were with older youth (19 through 23) who had spent more than six months on the streets. As a group, these youth were fairly knowledgeable about HIV. Most reported feeling very alienated from the mainstream service delivery system, and many told extremely painful stories of discrimination and abuse from mainstream service providers. Asked where they would go if they had a health problem, only 12 youth said they would turn to family or friends. Only 10 said they would visit a doctor or hospital. Few had attempted to enter drug treatment, and those who had entered treatment reported leaving within 48 hours.

In response to the dearth of available services, the youth described a help-seeking strategy that essentially involved shopping for services, eliciting help for one need in one program and help with another need from another program. This strategy grew out of frustration with the fact that no one program seemed to have the capacity to meet all their needs. They also feared being denied services because of particular aspects of their identity or behavior. For example, gay youth described feeling discriminated against on the basis of their sexual identity and having to hide their identity from some service providers. Similarly, youth who used drugs reported that they felt they had to conceal their drug use from some service providers. The fear of losing services or of being turned away from service providers was in some sense most pronounced among youth who reported previous exposure to the service delivery system, perhaps because the early life experiences of many of these youth included experiences of neglect and abuse.

Street youth also found that relying on one program was quite risky. The use of multiple programs generally meant that they were able to obtain more of what they felt they needed while they also reduced the risk that they would lose services if their relationship with any one program deteriorated. Health care, housing, and emergency food assistance were among the most pressing material needs they described in the interviews, although a considerable number emphasized that having someone trustworthy to talk to was the single most important benefit provided by outreach programs.

Relative to mainstream services, youth generally reported much greater confidence and trust in street outreach workers, including the health care services affiliated with outreach programs. Knowing the providers and being able to receive care on a regular schedule were cited as important factors. Youth preferred the sort of personal relationship afforded by outreach programs, as well as the overall atmosphere of the drop-in centers from which street outreach services emanated. These centers provided food, clothing, show-ers, general health care and family planning, and information on HIV, AIDS, and sexually transmitted diseases. Outreach programs also met emotional needs by providing a daytime respite from the streets, crisis intervention, and in many cases the only positive relationship with an adult that these youth had ever had. A strik-ing finding from these and subsequent ethnographic interviews was the centrality that outreach and drop-in center staff have in the emotional lives of these youth. We conducted an ethno-graphic exercise in which we asked youth to place themselves in the middle of a circle and to plot where various people were in terms of relative closeness to them. We expected youth to report family members or members of their peer group as closest to them. Surprisingly, many youth placed an outreach worker or drop-in center counselor as the person to whom they felt closest. They explicitly described feeling far greater trust and confidence in these individuals than in their family or peers.

Despite these positive feelings, however, youth described frus-tration and discouragement with the limited number of services available to them in outreach programs, noting that services were not available every day and often not when most needed. Youth also felt that many service providers were overburdened with cases. Many youth became attached to particular staff members and described difficulties in maintaining their relationship with a service program when that staff member left. In many cases, a change in staff was cited as one of the primary reasons for drop-ping out of services.

In summary, there was startling coherence among the admin-istrators, frontline service providers, and the youth themselves in terms of the inadequacy of the existing service delivery system. Although street outreach services and specialized drop-in centers seemed to respond well to street youth, the capacity of these pro-grams to meet the scope and complexity of the needs of these youth was clearly inadequate.

## Overview of Survey Findings

The findings of the CAP provided a rich foundation for developing a focus for subsequent activities, but the nature of the process limited the generalizability of the findings. We still did not know the degree to which street outreach reached this large and complex population or what impact outreach had on HIV risk reduction. Consequently, the next phase of the project involved the development of a carefully designed empirical study of street youth that was aimed at providing us with a demographic and behavioral profile as well as their contact with prevention-oriented services.

Historically, much of the available empirical information about street youth in New York City derived from a limited number of anecdotal studies of youth recruited in homeless shelters, foster care, drug treatment programs, and the criminal justice system. The inferences that could be drawn from these data were quite limited: The many youth who do not utilize shelter and drug treatment services were not represented. Youth in settings such as foster care and homeless shelters often conceal their identity and involvement in high-risk behaviors.

In an effort to overcome some of these limitations, a street-based sampling procedure was developed, based on ethnographic research conducted in natural settings where youth are known to congregate and participate in the street economy, such as bus and train stations, prostitution strolls, drug-copping sites, and areas in and around pornography shops, hustler bars, and public sex venues. Structured interviews were conducted with more than 900 street youth between February 1993 and July 1994. This was the first street-based sample of the homeless youth population of New York City. Youth included in the sample were between the ages of 12 and 23 and homeless and/or known to be dependent on the street economy as their primary means of economic support. Homelessness was defined as living on the streets in a squat, shelter, abandoned building, or some other type of public location that was a stable and safe living environment. The street economy included illegal activities like drug dealing and prostitution and quasi-legal activities like panhandling.

The majority of the youth were male. More than two thirds identified themselves as ethnic minorities, primarily black or Latino. At least a third identified themselves as gay, lesbian, or bisexual. Nearly half were living on the streets and sleeping in parks, subways, bus stations, and abandoned buildings. Two thirds of these had been on the streets for more than one year. In contrast to popular images of homeless youth who had come from distant locations, most of the youth were from the New York City metropolitan area. (To understand more about these youth, refer to our 1999 published ethnographic and demographic profiles of them in the suggested readings at the end of this chapter.)

Living on and from the streets, a precarious and often violent environment, these youth did what they could to stay afloat amid few economic options. Often this meant exchanging sex for money, food, shelter, and drugs. More than a third of the youth in the sample panhandled. Nearly a quarter were involved in the distribution of illegal drugs. About a quarter acknowledged being involved in prostitution, which is probably a substantial underestimate, given the stigmatizing nature of the term and the fact that sex work among these youth is often less commodified than among adult populations—frequently involving nonmonetary exchanges of sex for shelter, food, and drugs.

Youth reported high levels of drug use, including cocaine, amphetamines, crack, heroin, and LSD. Nearly a third had injected drugs, and roughly half of these had shared needles and other injection paraphernalia. Less than a quarter had ever been in drug treatment. Street outreach was shown to be an extremely effective conduit to the use of key prevention services, such as HIV testing and counseling, drug treatment, and STD screening and treatment. However, only about a fifth of the youth surveyed had ever had any contact with outreach services, reflecting the severe lack of resources targeted to this population.

## ENHANCEMENT OF OUTREACH SERVICES
## TARGETED TO STREET YOUTH

The development and implementation of the intervention occurred as an outgrowth of intensive dialogue with the service providers and youth themselves; this process required a substantial investment of time. It also required allowing the providers themselves be part of the decision-making and implementation process. Service providers were intimately involved in each and every decision; indeed, many of the core ideas came from the service providers themselves. A central problem from the outset, however, was developing a basis for trust between researchers and service providers— and, indeed, among service providers themselves. Many service providers had had bad experiences with research and were fearful of evaluation. Moreover, historically many of these programs had been competing among themselves for scarce resources, and there were also substantial philosophical differences between programs regarding priorities and modes of service delivery. Some of the key personnel involved had managed to forge effective working relationships with their counterparts in other agencies serving street youth, but others had not. Some immediately saw the need for establishing a means of working together; others were reticent. The process required a substantial investment of time and energy from all the key players.

Having established agreement on the broad parameters of the project with senior management staff from each agency involved, we brought together the key management staff with direct responsibility for supervising the day-to-day activities of each of the programs. The senior researcher outlined the broad objectives of the study and some of the potential directions that the project might take, and then left the process open for relatively free-ranging discussion and exploration of complementary or possibly competing options. Generally, management staff were quite receptive to the findings that had emerged from both the CAP and the survey research, and it was in and through discussion of the issues raised in the research that directions for the project unfolded. Interestingly, many of those who had initially approached the meetings with skepticism and perhaps saw them as yet another burden became quite enthusiastic about the prospect of working together in building an interagency network of service providers to work with street youth. Our team discovered that allowing the outreach programs to have control over this process was critical to the success of this phase.

This group, however, did not have a strong history of working together. Thus, there was a need to develop both an impetus and a mechanism for fostering communication and collective decision making among service providers. Much like the outreach process itself, the most effective way to establish the basis for communication and trust was to be responsive to the needs of the providers themselves. Based on the findings from the formative research, as well as on ongoing dialogue with the providers, we reached three broad conclusions that became the focus of the subsequent activities in the project. First, it was apparent that the size and complexity of the population in need far exceeded the capacity of the existing, highly fragmented group of programs that targeted street youth. Given the fact that there was little prospect for any expansion in fiscal resources, there was an urgent need to coordinate outreach services among the various programs at different agencies to maximize their efficiency. Second, service providers were confronted with very complex service delivery needs and required additional skills training to provide better care for homeless youth. Third, there was an urgent need to develop better documentation systems, both within programs and at the communitywide level. More reliable documentation of the needs and service delivery for this population would assist both case management and community planning for homeless youth.

## Coordination of Street Outreach Services

The community assessment process conducted in the beginning of the project indicated an overwhelming need to coordinate services among multiple programs. Perhaps more fundamentally, however, there was a clear need to build better systems of communication between programs so that a variety of activities could be more efficiently organized. For example, different programs were sending their outreach workers to the same geographic areas at the same time, creating a wasteful overlap of services. Meanwhile, other areas were left with little or no coverage at all. Programs shifted geographic coverage and times on the streets in response to movements in the population or in funding, often unaware of the same changes made by other programs. Many youth sought drop-in center services from two or more agencies, often resulting in conflicting and duplicate case management activities and a compounding of the problem of scarce resources. There was no interagency coordination of case management, service provision, or planning.

Outreach workers also reported that they frequently ran out of necessary outreach materials such as money for food, condoms, and bleach kits because of the sheer numbers of youth they found on the streets. These staff indicated that certain groups of youth were not being reached by services; they expressed personal frustration about not being able to do anything to meet these needs. Explanations for why some youth were missed included being outside a given program's geographic scope and staff's perceptions that some youth were too difficult to engage. In general, however, the greatest barrier was perceived to be the lack of resources to expand services. This point highlighted the need for a coordinated approach to service delivery to increase both the reach and efficiency of these services. In reviewing information from the interviews, we found that the service providers' perception that street youth were underserved was validated by the street-based surveys. Only about 20% of the youth surveyed reported having had contact with an outreach worker, confirming that the need for services far outstripped the capacity to provide such services. Given this information, the question for the service agencies was how to increase coverage at a time when no new resources were to be made available.

As part of the YAR project, representatives from each of the participating service agencies began meeting monthly to consider how they could better integrate the services provided by individual programs. At the beginning of each meeting, service providers shared information about what they had been doing in the previous month, the changes they had noticed in the population, and whether changes in service delivery had occurred. Gradually, the exchange of information evolved into an interest in coordinating services. The desire to do so was, at least in part, a response to feeling overwhelmed by the scope and complexity of needs within the street youth population, including the need for intensive AIDS risk-reduction interventions. At the same time, most agencies witnessed a decrease in the resources available for supporting HIV prevention services.

Meetings continued over the course of a year. Representatives discussed ways to collectively redistribute outreach resources to provide more complete coverage, especially in areas identified as having youth with little contact with any AIDS prevention services. A number of changes in the distribution of outreach services occurred. Outreach schedules were adjusted to accommodate greater coverage in certain areas or at certain times of the day. For example, we found that no services were available early in the day in midtown Manhattan. One of the agencies was able to change its schedule and open its facility earlier in the day, thus spreading the same resources across a longer time span and maximizing the overall coverage in this area. Some drop-in centers were able to coordinate activities across projects, which reduced duplication of services and brought about more effective mechanisms for informing youth about opportunities available at the different program sites. The individual projects also began to coordinate their special events, which they held on a regular basis, usually around holidays.

A substantial shift in resources took place in a section of the East Village frequented by youth at very high risk but not receiving outreach services of any kind. We convened a special meeting to address this issue. Based on our ethnographic and survey data, we provided a demographic and behavioral profile of the youth in this area to the service agencies. Our information indicated that they were almost all homeless, tended to be white, and had particularly high rates of injection drug use. The participants at this meeting concluded that there was a need to begin a specific outreach effort in the East Village. It was determined that each agency would divert a small part of its resources on a regular and sustained basis to provide better coverage in that area. For example, one agency, which had previously made visits to the area about once a month, increased the frequency of its East Village outreach to once a week. Similarly, another agency began to send at least one outreach team to the area each week. A third program, which had recently relocated its drop-in center nearby, began to provide extensive coverage of the East Village area. This increase in coverage was accomplished without increases in resources. Indeed, during this time, several of the projects were confronted with substantial budget cuts. On reviewing available data, we determined that outreach services actually increased during this time, despite the decrease in resources for HIV prevention and other services.

## Training

In our extensive interviews with outreach workers—the first point of contact with youth in crisis—we discovered that they received little, if any, specialized training for the work they do and were often left to devise their own techniques for working on the streets. This particular approach to problem solving had led to many outstanding, innovative outreach techniques specially tailored to the particular needs of homeless youth. However, there were significant drawbacks to this haphazard form of on-the-job training. It sometimes resulted in a trial-and-error approach to delivering outreach services, with reduced effectiveness, diminished job satisfaction, and high rates of staff burnout and turnover. Lack of training also resulted in inconsistencies in interventions used and HIV risk-reduction messages delivered. Like health education in general, consistency of message over time is a crucial element of effective HIV risk reduction; its lack can undercut even the most intensive and ardent efforts at service provision.

Specialized training for street outreach workers on issues related to their daily work was a crucial but largely missing piece of the street outreach picture. As discussed in Chapter 1, outreach workers' needs are unique because they function on the streets, in the scene, and on the turf of the target population, as opposed to having their clients come to them. Because they are frontline workers, they must win the trust of street youth, who may be extremely suspicious of adults, helping professionals, and other authority figures. Outreach workers not only offer tangible aid such as food, condoms, and subway tokens to destitute youth but also provide crisis intervention and a point of entry to needed services such as medical care, shelter, and drug treatment. Outreach workers also function as positive role models for these young people, many of whom have had difficult relationships with adults, including neglect, abuse, and exploitation.

The YAR senior staff agreed that we needed to establish a training program for the outreach staff of all the agencies working with us. We met with outreach workers and other staff, in an open forum context, to gain knowledge about their training needs before we devised the curriculum. In designing training sessions, we planned a curriculum that would enhance skills in several fundamental ways. First, it was vital to establish a greater degree of consistency in the skill level of staff within and across various agencies, particularly in relation to the rapidly evolving area of HIV treatment and care. The skills we wanted to address included street-based counseling techniques centered on drugs, AIDS, sexuality, and medical concerns such as tuberculosis; networking with key staff in service agencies and medical facilities; responding to street-based medical emergencies; advocating for youth; and providing emotional care and support. We also wished to educate outreach workers concerning HIV infection, AIDS, the complex mix of service issues related to this epidemic, and basic AIDS education to ensure that messages regarding HIV prevention were consistent across agencies.

Finally, we recognized that outreach staff had limited training in various theoretically derived intervention models. We wanted to include a conceptual foundation for the information and skills training, but many of the existing models were contradictory to the kinds of services and therapeutic relationships youth needed. In a 1996 study, we found that the Harm Reduction Model (HRM) served this function, providing both a clinical perspective and a therapeutic tool. First developed in the mid-1980s to reduce the harm associated with injection drug use, this strategy has since been extended to a wide number of at-risk populations and clinical applications. (Examples of these different uses of the HRM can be found in publications listed in the suggested readings.)

For the purposes of this discussion, a number of salient features of the HRM can be identified. As a public health strategy, the HRM recognizes that some behavioral outcomes have greater urgency than others and that the prevention of HIV transmission is the highest priority. As a risk-reduction strategy, the HRM is based on the recognition that HIV prevention goals must be tailored to specific needs and real-life capacities of the targeted individuals. The HRM provides risk-reduction education and tools to enable an individual to make the most health-promoting choices possible in a particular place and time. The HRM contrasts with other approaches that rely on coercion, penalty, and criminalization to change health-related behavior. Finally, as suggested by our 1997 study, HRM is based on the conviction that those to whom an intervention is being directed should have voice and power in the therapeutic process in which they are participating.

The training sessions were organized and directed by Edith Springer, ACSW, a clinical social worker and experienced trainer in the areas of drug abuse and AIDS. The key topics covered in these sessions are listed in Figure 5-1. A clinical psychologist assisted in the training on sexuality, and the session on health and medicine was led by a physician. Following completion of the training program, a harm reduction resource guide was developed. The resource guide was aimed at providing staff with ongoing support and giving new staff a background in both the nature of the street youth population and the use of the HRM. The resource guide summarized the empirical findings from the study and then provided detailed treatment of several of the key clinical issues commonly confronted by outreach staff who work with street youth: sexuality, substance abuse, prostitution, and violence. It also addressed the complex health issues confronting street youth: HIV, sexually transmitted diseases, tuberculosis, poor nutrition, and hepatitis.

**FIGURE  5-1     Youth at Risk: Key Topics for Training**

---

I. Introduction: A brief history of the development of outreach services for street youth in New York City

II. Overview of population and risk factors
  A. Demographic profile of New York City street youth
  B. Behavioral profile of youth

III. Why the harm reduction model?
  A. Overview of harm reduction model
  B. Harm reduction guidelines
  C. Harm reduction and street youth
  D. Instituting harm reduction: policy issues for the organization

IV. Key issues in harm reduction and street outreach
  A. Where street outreach meets harm reduction: the process-oriented approach
  B. Helping youth to make changes: approaches to intervention
  C. Why street outreach?
  D. Key characteristics of an outreach worker
  E. Issues in program design

V. Adolescent/street youth and drug use: an overview
  A. Factors associated with drug use among street youth
  B. The spectrum of substance use
  C. Key terms and concepts
  D. A new framework for understanding drug use
  E. Drug treatment: options and issues
  F. Methods for reducing the harm associated with drug use
  G. Techniques for working with substance-using youth

VI. Medical issues for street youth: an overview
  A. Medical needs and the outreach worker
  B. HIV/AIDS
  C. Sexually transmitted diseases
  D. Tuberculosis
  E. Gynecological care
  F. Family planning and pregnancy care
  G. Asthma
  H. Scabies

*(continued)*

**FIGURE 5-1**   *Continued*

---

   I.  When to call an ambulance

   J.  Health considerations for transgender youth

 VII.  Sex, sexuality, and sex work: an overview

     A.  Overview of adolescent sexuality and sexual development

     B.  Gay, lesbian, bisexual, and transgender youth

     C.  The impact of post-traumatic stress disorder

     D.  Sex work and survival sex

VIII.  Conclusion

---

## Evaluation of the Training Sessions

Our team thought it was important to evaluate and document the effects of the training sessions. The evaluation consisted of self-administered questionnaires completed at the beginning and end of each training session. Every question addressed an issue that was covered in the training session. There were four kinds of questions:

- Those assessing concrete knowledge (e.g., referral sources, knowledge of kinds of street drugs and illnesses)
- Those assessing theoretical knowledge of harm reduction
- Simulated problem solving to indicate understanding of the outreach strategy
- Questions evaluating the utility and responsiveness of the training from the trainee's viewpoint

Thirty-three outreach workers participated in our training sessions, about 95% of the relevant staff. The average age of the outreach workers from YAR cooperative agencies who attended the 1995 training series was 31, and two thirds were women. About two thirds had been outreach workers for less than 3 years, and about the same proportion were college graduates.

A fairly high level of knowledge was demonstrated on the tests before training; improvement occurred primarily on conceptual material relating to adolescent psychosocial development, rather than on sources of referrals, concrete knowledge, and other knowledge about service activities. More than 90% of the participants found the curriculum "very relevant" to their work with street youth, and the same percentage of participants felt they would use what they learned "a fair amount" or "extensively" in their work. One of the unexpected consequences of the training was that virtually all staff reported that the training provided a unique opportunity to meet other providers who work with street youth, share common problems, and strategize about potential solutions. Over the course of the project, the training evolved into an interagency team-building exercise for the community of providers that helped to relieve some of the feelings of isolation and helplessness that many felt in struggling to meet the demands of their jobs.

It was our conclusion that providing training for outreach workers significantly enhanced the conceptual knowledge and skills on specific topics, like drug abuse and adolescent sexuality, that are central to work with street youth. Such training is successful and should be seen as a necessary aspect of outreach, given the high rate of staff turnover in this stressful and often low-paying job.

## DEVELOPMENT OF A COMPUTERIZED
## NETWORK FOR YOUTH SERVICES

One of the most significant accomplishments of the YAR project was the establishment and maintenance of a computer-based system that linked its member service organizations. This system, which is still in place, reduced many of the problems identified in the earlier phases of the project: It helped to reduce service overlap, maintain more comprehensive records on youth, improve service coverage, and coordinate the efforts of many geographically diffuse agencies. In developing the computer system, we faced technological obstacles as well as cultural barriers, such as fear of technology among both service providers and youth.The process gave us insight into some issues involved in providing services for a marginalized population that we might not have recognized otherwise. We believe that the story of how we developed this system

and the challenges we faced in making it work can instruct anyone who wants to think about linking service providers by using
technology. Specifically, we wanted to use this technology to (1)
systematically document a wide range of prevention services at
the agency level, (2) facilitate the exchange of case management
and service delivery information between agencies, and (3)
develop a system for documenting existing and emerging service
delivery needs at the community level.

The computer system developed for the YAR project involved
the creation of a local area network (LAN) within each individual
agency as well as a wide area network (WAN) among the agencies. A database at each site allowed individual counselors to
record a wide range of information about case management and
service delivery activities, and a computer network allowed counselors from different agencies to exchange information about
youth who are receiving services from more than one agency. We
also developed an electronic mail system for disseminating schedule changes, program announcements, and updates within and
among agencies and a standardized outreach report (as well as
other reports) to facilitate collection of data on outreach and case
management services on a community-wide level.

At the level of the individual case worker, the system provided
a uniform template for recording a wide range of demographic,
case management, and service delivery information. The WAN
facilitated the exchange of service-oriented information among
the YAR programs, particularly around services that were directly
related to HIV prevention, such as medical care, housing, and
drug treatment. The creation of a parallel database in each of the
project sites enabled us to document every case within the programs, replacing much of the record keeping that was done on
paper with computer software that simultaneously functioned as
case management, case tracking, and services documentation.
This system made it possible for counselors in different programs
to know what kinds of services youth were receiving elsewhere,
what types of appointments had been made, and what attempts
had been made to secure housing, drug treatment, or other needed
services. This tracking system substantially reduced a major prob-

lem we had documented earlier in the project, namely, the duplication of services. It also increased the overall efficiency of the service
delivery system. By streamlining the delivery system, resources were
redirected toward providing direct services, resulting in a greater
number of higher quality services, delivered in a more consistent,
coordinated, and coherent manner. This, in turn, enhanced the ability of the service agencies to assist youth in making sustained behavioral changes with respect to HIV risk reduction. The parallel project
databases also provided a communitywide database that was
employed to document the frequency and distribution of services for
the street youth population at the community level, information
that enabled the agencies of the YAR cooperative to plan and
develop service delivery strategies more effectively at this level.

## Problems in Establishing the Wide Area Network

However, we did encounter some difficulties in establishing the
WAN. In general, the following problem areas were encountered
as the WAN moved from the planning stage to the implementation phase. We present them in the order in which they occurred.

### Software Selection

In implementing any computerized system, decisions concerning
software logically precede the hardware selections. A key decision
in software selection is choosing between an existing system (and
modifying it to fit the organization's needs) or developing a new
system from scratch (using a compiled package such as Paradox).
The main advantage of building a new system is the flexibility
and responsiveness to changing needs that a tailored system
affords. However, the disadvantage of hiring an expert program-
mer to create and maintain a WAN is that the system is dependent on this individual (or someone of comparable expertise) to
maintain it. Cost also plays a major role in the decision because
the price of an existing software package is initially large but
known, whereas the costs of developing a new system gradually
accumulate, and the total expense cannot be reliably predicted at
the outset.

Because the money allotted for the WAN was a preestablished lump sum that could not be increased, and because previously compiled software offered the advantage of having a fully operational system in a relatively short time, the YAR cooperative agencies decided that buying an existing software package would be the best choice. We conducted an extensive review of existing packages, comparing technical features, flexibility, cost, and technical support services. We did this in the early 1990s, and since then workshops have been developed that provide much of this information to prospective buyers, including a review of more than 40 such software packages, complete with comparative ratings of each.

### Hardware Selection

If possible, we suggest that the vendor chosen to provide software should also choose the hardware to support the software or at least be included in the process of hardware selection. In our case, this process became complicated by the fact that no one had the necessary background to know which configuration was best. Involvement by the software company was essential in helping us select the proper hardware configuration.

Issues also arose pertaining to the procurement of dedicated phone lines, office space, and electrical outlets to support the addition of this system. Modems installed at each site were used to communicate between agencies and the central server, where back-ups and related activities were conducted. Both data entry and usage of the system were impeded by a shortage of computers. Because in most cases several staff members will need to access data simultaneously, a LAN at each participating agency was a necessity.

### Fostering an Effective Dialogue with Software Vendors

A typical problem with establishing a computerized case management system is that for a software company to write appropriate code for an agency's needs, the agency is required to detail explicitly what is necessary for their system. This obliges the agency's staff to view their own functions from the point of view of a computer software developer—and we found this was not an easy task! The agencies involved gathered all the documents and reports that were currently in use or planned for use and detailed the data necessary for all of them.

Formulating specified coding and common variables between agencies turned out to be perhaps the greatest difficulty. It was essential to create computerized variables, yet agency staff usually do not think in terms of the universe of responses or categories involved in data collection for research purposes. For instance, the variable of "sexual identity" required several hours of discussion as to whether the codes should be limited to heterosexual, homosexual, and bisexual or expanded to distinguish between gay and lesbian. The questions of whether to include transgenders, cross-dressers, and transsexuals as separate codes and whether to base the sexual identity designations on behavior (e.g., men who have sex with men but self-identify as heterosexual) were also debated at length. Prior to computerization, agency staff would simply record whatever a youth said, or what they knew about the youth's behavior, and would not have assigned codes. The same is true for demographic variables like race, in that ethnicity may or may not be included, and people of mixed race may be described or listed as "other." Codes for extremely complex variables like "presenting problem" or "service type" were even more troublesome.

Another problem involved the terminology commonly used by people who know computers, requiring staff on the program side to be familiar with terms like *megabytes, RAM, batch files,* and *footprints.* Explanations of these matters to individuals with little or no computer involvement are never easy to deliver or to understand. A tremendous amount of patience and perseverance—on all parts—was necessary to achieve understanding because no one person in the decision-making group had all the necessary pieces of information to reach conclusions. It was very helpful to hire a software vendor based in the same geographic area as the WAN.

### Computer Phobia
Many project staff who were required to use the computer system had little or no prior experience with computers and, in some

cases, were resistant to the very idea of computerizing client records. The fear that the computer system would be used as a way of monitoring or supervising agency staff was but one aspect of the anxiety related to computerization. In addition, staff were afraid of "breaking" the computer system by doing something wrong with it. There were also personal concerns and insecurities about possessing the necessary intelligence or skill to do computer work, and there were fears that the computer system would be overly technical, confusing to use, and generally inaccessible.

In familiarizing staff with the use of the hardware and the case management software, training was conducted without assuming any prior experience with computers, alleviating many of the staff's fears. Training focused on making sure that data were put in the right places, that data fields were not skipped, and that data were not inadvertently deleted. This was accomplished by

## Choosing Software

In determining which system will be most appropriate, some of the major questions to be asked of any potential software company or vendor include, at minimum, the following:

What kinds of reports can the system generate? Can these reports be customized?

Is the system capable of holding extensive narrative (e.g., case notes on individual clients)?

Is there ease of screen presentation, data entry, movement between screens, "help" functions, and other commonly used features?

What operating system does the software require?

What are the system's backup and security arrangements?

What kind of training and technical support exist, and are they included in the basic cost of the system? Does technical assistance include hands-on training as well as ongoing telephone or modem-based support? How quickly does the software company respond when training and technical support are needed?

Does the purchaser receive a copy of the source codes, user's guides, or other texts?

How is licensing of the software accomplished (i.e., via buying, leasing, or some other arrangement)? Who has the right to change the software if necessary?

Does the software vendor have prior experience working with a multisite configuration and complicated data security issues between projects? Can the vendor provide good references from these other projects?

Does the software vendor have systems for recording all relevant data? If not, is it possible to obtain these systems, and how much will this cost?

Does the software interface with other kinds of software (e.g., statistical packages and word processing)?

Does the software require expensive hardware as a result of utilizing considerable storage space or working memory or running only on the latest chips? At what speed does the software perform various operations with various kinds of hardware?

acquiring a system that automatically safeguards against data deletion. Directions and prompts on each screen and system-generated "save" prompts and "not saved" warnings are also helpful. In addition, we found it helpful to create a user-friendly manual that can be used by staff to self-train on both LAN and WAN systems, thus minimizing training and retraining costs. Designated "computer literate" staff and clearly written documentation of computer usage are essential in service environments where there tends to be considerable staff turnover.

An additional set of problems involved how youth perceived our computerized case management system. Some young people perceived the computer technology as an instrument of control or the emblem of an oppressive society. There was concern that the computer system could contribute to feelings of intimidation or alienation among clients at the drop-in centers or that young people would worry about becoming "just another number" or statistic in the system. These fears seemed to dissipate as the system became a normal, ongoing part of life at the various sites. The YAR personnel and the project directors at each agency emphasized that the attitude emanating from the program staff would in large part set the tone for whether youth perceived the computer system as helpful or harmful.

### Confidentiality Issues

Case management involves the entry, storage, and retrieval of highly confidential information. Agency personnel feared that "hackers" or other unauthorized individuals might somehow be able to tap into the system, destroying valuable data or making confidential data known to outsiders. These concerns were heightened in the context of HIV-related information, particularly among the medical providers who represented one of the participating agencies.

These kinds of fears are real for people, even if they are sometimes based on misconceptions. Working through these concerns requires time and patience at every level. We pointed out to staff members that their old systems of hard copy documents in file cabinets were probably more vulnerable to theft than the new computerized system. We also noted that someone would have to know the unlisted phone number to dial in through a modem or would have to forcibly enter the building and break through complex password systems to access the data without a modem.

Staff at the outreach projects also expressed their concerns that some type of technical difficulty might result in the erasure or destruction of the data storage mechanisms. This worry provided opportunities to reinforce the importance of backing up the data from the system on separate diskettes or tape-drive devices. Other precautions taken against theft and data loss included protecting all tapes, diskettes, and drives with locks and/or passwords. Two layers of passwords were required to access YAR data, and the modem phone number, as previously stated, was unlisted. In addition, the risk of computer theft was minimized by securing or fastening computers to desks and/or keeping them in locked rooms.

Because the system was designed for interagency use, service providers worried that confidential information could be accessed by unauthorized staff at other agencies. Clearly, to reduce duplication of services, each agency needed to know which services other agencies were offering to a given client. However, describing these services in detail often disclosed other information that youth and their counselors might not want to divulge. For instance, some types of housing services are available only to individuals who are HIV-positive. Indicating that this service is being used reveals a client's HIV status by default. Similarly, one of the YAR agencies specializing in services for gay and lesbian youth expressed the concern that it would be assumed that anyone receiving services from this agency was gay or lesbian, leaving them vulnerable to potential discrimination. Other sensitive information, such as whether the client has a history of drug abuse or has been sexually or physically abused, clearly needed protection as well.

The YAR participants finally decided that "sharable" information would consist of basic demographic characteristics and some specified broad categories of services. Consensus was reached through a series of meetings in which we outlined 10 categories of service. These categories were kept very broad (e.g., "entitlements" or "housing") and were designed so that other YAR participating agencies would know that a service requested by a youth was being delivered elsewhere, without revealing any of the specifics about that service. To avoid duplicating that service, the worker would contact the other agency by phone or e-mail, procure a consent from the youth to access the other agency's files on that youth, and find out the specifics of the service being rendered.

The project director and the clinical director at each agency were given the maximum degree of access to client records. At the agency level, they determined which staff received access to which aspects of the system. In most instances, the projects did not restrict each counselor's access to their individual case load because, although youth at some projects were assigned a primary counselor, they were often seen by other counselors or staff. Access levels were recognized by the utilization of user passwords.

### Consent Issues

The issue of obtaining written, signed, and time-limited consent forms from youth to reveal case information was discussed at length at a YAR interagency training. This training included a review of the city, state, and federal regulations under which a social worker, counselor, social services worker, or health care worker is obligated to obtain written consent to release any information. A mechanism was established within the computer system to allow youth to designate which other agencies within the YAR cooperative were providing services and whether they would consent to allowing general information about them to be transmitted to that agency.

Two levels of consent were used in the system. At the outset, for example, a girl could decide that she wants case data shared with only some and not all of the participating agencies, so that if she dislikes a particular agency, she could exclude it from having any access to her files. At this level of consent, demographics and one of 10 service categories would be the only information shared. For a provider to obtain anything else, the youth must give additional consent.

During the intake process, some youth hesitated to consent to having their case information shared with other providers, even though counselors had been encouraged to make it clear to youth that many security measures had been built into the system. The ongoing problem with obtaining consent from the youth to share data with other agencies did show signs of improvement, as more youth agreed to consent over time. Much of the problem may have been unease among outreach staff themselves rather than among the youth, although this was difficult to ascertain. There was a common client view that if the need arose, they would give consent, rather than giving it initially.

### Documentation Issues and Professionalism

As mentioned earlier, the documentation process both within and among the YAR agencies varied considerably before computerization. There were several reasons for this difference, including different agency policies and procedures; different funding streams, each with its own reporting requirements; inadequate staff training in documentation procedures; lack of time and resources to do a thorough job of documenting cases; and wide variations among the skills and experience of individual staff members.

The WAN computer system focused attention on documentation issues much more intensely than the intermittent and hurried manner in which documentation is often viewed when a report is required or when a city or state funding official visits to examine records. Simply installing the WAN required a review of all client files so that data entry could proceed. During this process, gaps and overlaps in the documentation of services rendered to clients received a sustained examination. Some staff had not maintained adequate records, which may or may not reflect lapses in job performance because documentation has often been viewed as secondary to the crisis-oriented, client-focused work in which these agencies are involved. Thus, we stressed in training that documentation is essential in advocating for youth, because without it there is no record of client needs or the efforts to meet them.

The wide range of educational backgrounds among the agencies' staff members posed a variety of problems for the outreach projects' effective use of the computer system. Some staff had little or no prior experience with computers, or even with typing. At each agency, a few people had received additional training and functioned as the resident "computer experts." However, targeting a small group of staff to fulfill this function places an extra burden on them and can create conflicts between getting their own counseling or outreach work done and responding to the technological needs of their fellow staff. We had originally expected that all staff would be trained and fully equipped to comfortably utilize the computer system, but in practice the process of bringing everyone up to speed took longer than anticipated.

### Technical Support

Fortunately, in implementing and maintaining our WAN system, only minor and occasional problems have required professional technical support. One major advantage to a close working relationship between software and hardware vendors is that all technical support may be allocated to one or two vendors, rather than to several vendors who each may claim that another vendor is responsible for responding to a problem when trouble arises. As a precaution, we found it advisable to have a weekly monitoring system in place to eliminate out-of-range data, duplicate entries, and other confusing errors in the database.

## CONCLUSION

Based on a systems perspective, this chapter has described the Youth at Risk Project, a five-year study aimed at evaluating and enhancing street outreach services targeted to homeless youth in New York City and building a coherent infrastructure for HIV prevention services. Many of the anticipated results of this project were realized. For example, benefits from coordination of outreach activities included broader dissemination of information about the emerging needs and distribution of the population and greater geographic and temporal coverage by outreach. Even without additional resources, there was an increase in the numbers of youth contacted by outreach and a gain in efficiency. Benefits of our training program included greater understanding and communication between outreach programs and reduced staff burnout. Benefits of the computerized case management system included more efficient documentation of services within programs and more coherent case management between multiple programs serving the same individual. Although the particular needs of homeless youths and other at-risk populations will vary, as will the available resources with which to support needed services, in this case study we hope to have provided an example of what can be accomplished in using a systems perspective in program evaluation and development.

## SUGGESTED READINGS

Clatts, M. C., & Davis, W. R. (1999). A demographic and behavioral profile of homeless youth in New York City: Implications for AIDS outreach and prevention. *Medical Anthropology Quarterly, 10,* 105–114.

Clatts, M. C., Davis, W. R., & Atillasoy, A. (1995). Hitting a moving target: the use of ethnographic methods in the evaluation of AIDS outreach programs for homeless youth in NYC. In E. Y. Lambert, R. S. Ashery, & R. U. Needle (Eds.), *Qualitative methods in drug abuse and HIV research* (National Institute on Drug Abuse Research Monograph 157), pp. 117–135.

Clatts, M. C., Davis, W. R., Bresnahan, M., Springer, E., Backes, G., & Linwood, C. (1996). The Harm Reduction Model: An alternative approach to AIDS outreach and prevention among street youth in New York City. In P. Erickson, D. Riley, Y. Cheuny, & P. O'Hare (Eds.), *Harm reduction: A new direction for drug policies and programs.* Toronto: University of Toronto Press, pp. 393–409.

Clatts, M. C., Hillman, D. J., Atillasoy, A., & Davis, W. R. (1999). Lives in the balance: An ethnographic profile of homeless youth in New York City. In J. Bluestein & C. Levine (Eds.), *Medical decision-making for adolescents who are alone.* New York: Cambridge University Press.

Newcombe, R. (1990, April). *The reduction of drug-related harm: A conceptual framework for theory, practice and research.* Paper presented at the First International Conference on the Reduction of Drug-Related Harm, University of Liverpool, Liverpool, England.

Sorge, R. (1991). *Drug policy in the age of AIDS: The philosophy of "harm reduction."* National Alliance of Methadone Advocates Educational Series, No. 2. (Reprinted from *Health PAC Bulletin, 20,* 4–10.)

Springer, E. (1991). Effective AIDS prevention with active drug users: The HRM. *Journal of Chemical Dependency Treatment, 4,* 141–157.

Strang, J., Heathcote, S., & Watson, P. (1987). Habit moderation in injecting drug addicts. *Health Trends, 19,* 16–18.

Strang, J., & Farrell, M. (1992). Harm minimization for drug users: When second best may be best first. *British Medical Journal, 304,* 1127–1128.

# 6

# GIVING BACK TO THE COMMUNITY: PLAYING FAIR IN THE INFORMATION AND SERVICE EXCHANGE

BEATRICE J. KRAUSS, PH.D.

Every research project seeks to answer a set of important questions, and every service organization is guided by its mission statement. In well-run projects and programs, these goals are stated clearly and understood by everyone. When organizations are flexible and responsive to their constituencies, they are able to adjust their aims in response to changing conditions in the community. In this chapter, I outline the ways in which organizations can be more responsive to both the individuals in the communities they serve and the community as a whole. I recognize that developing strategies to make organizations more responsive is not a new issue. Techniques have been developed to accomplish this goal, and I review some of these strategies. Using my experiences in directing projects on the Lower East Side of New York City, a multicultural neighborhood with many active community-based health and social service organizations, I describe strategies that go further in terms of community responsiveness than the traditional techniques.

I also point out that, if our *clients' satisfaction* is the ultimate standard of our research and service endeavors, none of us knows enough in advance about clients to do our jobs well. We need to collaborate with our clients to gain their insights and cooperation before we even begin to work toward our goals. We cannot know enough about the cultural and historical context, personal biographies, resources, and strengths and weaknesses of clients unless we engage them and their community in an ongoing conversation. To illustrate, I have lived in Oregon, Ohio, Georgia, Kansas, Illinois, and Texas, but I now work with families on the Lower East Side of New York City on a project that combines research and service. I could neither design interviews, write questionnaires, plan programs, make referrals, nor interpret data without some cultural assistance from the children and adults of the Lower East Side. And that leaves us with a question—the central question of this chapter—if we get this assistance for our community-based projects, how are we going to pay for it and acknowledge it? In this chapter, I describe how our attention to the perceptions of our own clients, their suggestions, and their views of our place within the community has taught us that we can go further in assuring that a fair exchange takes place between organizations and the communities they serve. The result of our playing fair has led us to create an organization that does not just deliver services or conduct research in a community but over time becomes an integral part of it. As I will describe, many of the ways of giving back have been suggested by our clients and by the community-based organizations (CBOs) with which we work. I thank the members of the Lower East Side AIDS Strategy Group, a consortium of service providers on the Lower East Side, and the parents and children who have been participants in our projects, advisory boards, pilot studies, and focus groups for sharing their insights.

Before I begin to describe our experiences in "playing fair," I would like to note a few qualifications and limitations. Community-based organizations and research projects must satisfy many different and sometimes conflicting goals. The desire to provide client satisfaction can be mitigated by the demands of larger bureacracies, funding agencies, and civic ordinances. Although I recognize these conflicts and their ability to limit effectiveness, they are not the focus of this chapter. I prefer to focus on the interactions over which we have the most control—those between our agencies and the people they serve.

## DIFFERING PRIORITIES OF RESEARCHERS, PROVIDERS, AND CLIENTS

Through 10 years of experience in the field, I have read about or had clients tell me when our projects and programs make them feel short-changed. Whether we are a research organization or a service provider, we have a limited mission. We cannot do everything for our clients, and what we do may not be highest on our clients' list of needs. For example, perhaps we have come into the community with a mission to prevent HIV infection, but the clients sitting in front of us may need food for their children today or a place to stay right now. We may feel that giving the results of an HIV test is our highest public health priority, but the client may feel that having to confront the HIV test result—and what it means for her children's future—is not the highest immediate priority. She may need food for her children that day because her welfare check has been delayed and she has no money. If we fail to consider clients' immediate needs first, they may feel ignored and are, in fact, not being served adequately.

Research or service procedures may appear "impolite." In the course of our research projects, we ask very nosy questions about sex, drugs, and personal history, but we tell clients little about ourselves. We react differently when we hear someone got HIV through a transfusion than when we hear it was through drug use. We may interrupt an interview to take a phone call. We stick people with needles and ask people to pee in cups. We ask clients to adapt to our workday, but we do not adapt to theirs. Without an ongoing dialogue with our clients, we would not recognize these facts and how they may affect the success of our mission.

Experts may be perceived as "superior." Whether we are security guards, substance abuse counselors, or research consultants, we are perceived by clients as experts in some way. We know where things are in our office or building, the order in which things are likely to happen, and how much time things take, and we also have a fair idea of where the client's information goes. We are in our offices for a perfectly good reason—a legitimate job. We have some fair idea about how the clients' problems are going to be addressed.

Simply doing our jobs may make us seem to be acting "above" our clients. It is easy for us to think of clients as both uninformed or knowing more than they actually do. It is easy to put down their reasons for being "clients" rather than experts like us, easy to act as if we know more about their problems than they do, and easy to treat the "client" as something to study or serve rather than as an individual with a life that is as fully complicated and interesting as our own. The ability to experience this process as the client does could alert project staff to these problems.

Paperwork and intakes are perceived and experienced as annoying barriers. Clients expect service; they expect things to run smoothly. We give out messages that say, "Come see us and we'll make sure you get in a support group for HIV-positive people." In actuality, what we should have said is "Come see us, and if you remembered to bring form M11Q, which you had to see a doctor to get, and you read and sign this consent form, and you spend one and a half hours being interviewed for the research and intake because we need this data to apply for another grant and to meet the reporting requirements not only of our institution but also of our auditors, and we have an opening on a day that is convenient to you, because our other clients so far could meet only on Thursdays in the morning and Wednesdays in the evening, then you can have some social support in a week or two, because next week the person who runs the Wednesday group that you want is taking her vacation in accordance with the employee contract for our institution—that is, if you see a doctor and get an M11Q." These extra tasks and barriers, even the waiting, seem like "work," something the client has to get through to get paid with service or dollars or care. Clients often feel surprised and bewildered by the amount of work they must do to obtain a service.

Many communities have been exploited by research or service organizations in the past. Especially among the poor and marginalized, there is deep suspicion of the true motivations of organizations and institutions. In the past, incidents such as the Tuskegee trials—in which minority men were left untreated so that the natural history of syphilis could be observed—demonstrated that the lives of certain citizens were held cheaply by the U.S. Government's Public Health Service. As Thomas and Quinn wrote in 1991 in the *American Journal of Public Health,* researchers and service organizations often must compensate for this history by presenting important and convincing evidence that the client's interests have been taken to heart.

Research or service organizations may have an unintended negative impact on local communities. Through our projects, we gather information to prevent HIV infection among highly affected populations such as injection drug users. However, this goal is not perceived so clearly in the community. For example, at various times, we have been told by a community organization that we are taking clients away from them just as they are about to enter their door. In another instance, parents in the community reviewed a draft of an article I wrote and noted, "You are describing the neighborhood where I live as a 'center of sex and drug trade since the turn of the century'—what if my child reads this article?" Another client noted, "The CBO down the block only seems to hire Latino staff; they don't have any African Americans; nobody seems to come from the neighborhood; it's not a place that I or any of my African American friends feel comfortable going." In addition, our organization could be in competition with locally owned or operated organizations. It may displace a needed apartment, store, or doctor's office. It could draw strangers to the neighborhood who do not use neighborhood businesses. It may put extra pressure on scarce resources, such as parking or garbage pickup, but add no new jobs to the neighborhood. Often, projects provide needed services for a limited time and then dash hopes by leaving when funding runs out. Perhaps we should think about community impact in the same way that organizations have begun to document their environmental impact.

## TRADITIONAL METHODS OF IMPROVING RELATIONSHIPS WITH CLIENTS

Organizations have tried to address many of the problems mentioned. Based on my own experience, I describe some of the most common methods of addressing these issues. As mentioned previously, I have noticed that these methods often do not go far enough, as well intended as they are. They do not recognize that creating an equitable exchange between clients and CBOs requires a true balance between what each party in the exchange gets and receives.

### Needs Assessments

Community-based organizations generally try to be in harmony with stated and unstated community needs. Often, this is done by gathering data to illuminate the most pressing community concerns. To accomplish this, organizations can do face-to-face interviews or phone surveys to see if people want and need their programs, or they can conduct focus groups of community members. Ethnographic fieldwork, as described in Chapter 5, is another tool that can be used to identify community concerns. When focus groups are part of a needs assessment, participants are guided by a group leader to talk in a particular way about community needs. In addition, organizations can put together existing data from the census, hospital admissions, police records, a literature review, or other sources to identify a community's most pressing needs. Often, organizations involve community leaders or representatives in guiding and forming the needs assessment.

## Compensation

Organizations in touch with their clients try to structure their hours in accordance with the flow of their clients' lives—for example, being open on evenings or weekends. They also remove other barriers to clients' attendance. If their services are for parents with small children, they provide babysitting. If their catchment area is large and their clientele poor, they assist by providing transportation or covering the cost of public transportation. If clients must be present for long periods, they make food and drink available or provide it free to clients with little money. If they are asking clients for something—research information, for example— they pay clients for their time.

## Civility, Cultural Sensitivity, and Preparing Clients for Unexpected Burdens

Well-run organizations offer their staff training on delicate issues that are important to their mission. Topics for training can include, among others, confidentiality procedures for medical information and how to interview about intimate topics such as sexual practices or drug use. Some organizations require training on cultural diversity and cultural variations in polite forms of interchange. Direct eye contact, for example, is courteous in some cultures but insulting and disrespectful in others. Some organizations are committed to hiring staff who are multicultural or multilingual and who represent the diverse ethnic backgrounds of the community served.

The very best run organizations give clients videotapes, brochures, or illustrations that let them know exactly what to expect in advance and how to prepare for it. Two very different types of organizations have come a long way in this regard: moving companies and hospitals. The best moving companies give out step-by-step guides, organized by the months and weeks leading up to moving day. The guides suggest when to arrange to disconnect the phone, when to start packing the dishes, when to contact the school in the new neighborhood, what documents you should arrange to take to a new doctor or school, and what will happen on moving day. The best hospitals prepare patients for procedures and aftercare by similar step-by-step guides. In conversations with patients, the nurse covers everything about the procedure on a checklist; videos show exactly what to expect during treatment and how patients can assist in their own recovery. Hospitals may also provide illustrated storybooks and brochures that clients can use to brush up on important points. Some hospitals even have buddy or support programs in which volunteers who have been through similar procedures act as guides and helpers to the new patient.

## Evaluation

How can we keep the community updated about our progress? Are we evaluating the organization's work to demonstrate that it is meeting community needs? If things change in the community, can we adapt to the change? These questions imply that evaluation should be an ongoing process. However, needs assessments are typically conducted at the beginning of a project, and mechanisms are not usually in place to conduct ongoing evaluations.

## Staff from the Community

Many research and service organizations hire some community members as staff, and these people are often regarded as a "bridge" between the management of the organization and the clients. Staff from the community often meet the clients face to face as interviewers, receptionists, and security personnel. These staff members understand the language and culture of the community and can offer advice to upper management about pertinent community issues. But, if they are present only in the lower-level positions and not in the management of the project, what kind of message is the community getting? Does the community see upper management on a daily basis?

Some CBOs have community members among upper management or serving on advisory boards that help to keep senior management informed about community issues. Thus, most organizations get some information about the community from the "top" (advisory boards) and the "bottom" (frontline staff who have daily interaction with community members). Most of these tactics and strategies demonstrate that the community is welcome and included in the management and daily work of the project, but, as I will explain, these mechanisms do not go far enough.

## TO GIVE BACK TO THE COMMUNITY MORE EFFECTIVELY

In social psychological theory, fairness is achieved when all participants perceive a balance between what each is getting and giving. It is beneficial to periodically examine whether this balance exists in the relationships an organization has with clients, other CBOs in the community, and the community itself. If an organization collaborates with others, what do they get from the relationship? Are data being collected that will help them apply for their own funding? Are they getting to do joint projects? Regarding the clients served, are those who give the organization insights on how to do the job better getting anything in return? For example, are they getting employment opportunities? Are they getting appropriate referrals to other services they may need? Do they have a place on the advisory board?

In assessing the balance in the relationship between the two parties, there is a tendency to overvalue what the organization is putting in and undervalue what others, in this case, the community or clients, are putting in. We see others from the outside and ourselves from the inside. To overcome the inclination to undervalue others' contributions, it is necessary to recognize that we learn the most from people who experience things differently. Clients, likewise, have a lot to learn from the organization. To facilitate mutual understanding among clients, the larger community, and the organization, we advocate taking advantage of the many opportunities for face-to-face conversation and interaction. Whether the organization is new to a community, redefining its mission, or assessing progress, small groups and one-on-one conversations are the most valuable first steps. An initial conversation can center on a key issue in achieving balance; that is, what do we each have to put into our relationship?

## From Needs Assessment to Needs Dialogue

Community members and CBOs often ask the following questions about each other: What do we have to offer each other? What problems do we have? How can we help solve them together? As Seth Kalichman has reminded us, researchers, especially in the social sciences, are often surprised to learn that CBOs and community members do not really know what social scientists do. People think psychologists, for example, either give therapy or do evaluations. They think other kinds of scientists—for example, epidemiologists—only do huge surveys to uncover problems. They often do not know that social scientists have a variety of useful skills: They have command of a large research literature on programs that work and do not work. They can design research projects to answer questions important to the community. They can use the information they collect to develop theories about human behavior and, in turn, use these theories to design programs and projects to meet community needs. When influencing policy makers is necessary, they understand statistics and can use their data to make effective arguments. They can also use their knowledge of research design and statistics to sift through large amounts of competing claims of success; they write grants, articles, and books. Finally, they have some expertise in how organizations work.

Fairness also comes into play in the relationship between CBOs. Those located in the same community often do not have a clear idea about the services each offers or the special equipment or special experts on staff that each has. They often worry that they are in competition over scarce funding, thinking anything that benefits another CBO will hurt theirs. The CBO staff know about designing and administering program budgets, the pressures of running several programs, and serving clients with multiple problems. If they have a good record-keeping system, they are also aware of the most common presenting problems in the community within any given time period.

The expertise of the clients themselves often goes untapped. We seldom consider that clients know what it is like to step through the door of our organization, go through our procedures, and live or work in the neighborhood where our organization is located. They have a perspective on neighborhood problems and a feeling as to whether they got help with their problems at particular organizations. They are experts on many issues that are of direct concern to us and our organization.

Each of these constituencies has skills or information to offer the other. Social scientists need to know about neighborhood life and what needs are met or ignored by CBOs; CBOs need to know if they have overlapping or nonoverlapping programs, if they have a good reputation in the neighborhood, if their programs are working well, and if they should establish new programs that would work better. They also need to pay attention to maintaining a balance between organizational efficiency and providing client services. Clients need to know they are going to the best places to meet a particular need and to understand that what each client may believe is his or her own individual problem really affects many other people.

## Performing an Assessment of Programming

Abby Wasserman, a social scientist, has devised guidelines for assessing a CBO. He lists eight questions about programming that CBOs should ask themselves and points out that these are best answered in collaboration with social scientists. To answer some of the questions, the social scientists, in turn, need the clients. Here are the questions Wasserman suggests we use in assessing a particular program's place in the community:

1. Is the program meeting a high-priority need?
2. Why should this intervention (program) be chosen over others to address that need?

3. How does this intervention fit with other programming?
4. Can the CBO carry out this intervention?
5. How well is the CBO doing this intervention?
6. Does the intervention work?
7. Can it be improved?
8. Can it become a regular part of the organization?

Finding a social scientist and client experts to assist in this assessment may require conducting searches and interviews, as an organization would recruit an employee. To get them to talk together, forming an organization may be necessary, like the Lower East Side AIDS Strategy Group. This is a group of service providers, client representatives, and researchers who meet monthly to assure that AIDS-related community needs are being addressed and that different organizations in the community are not stepping on others' toes. Another strategy for providing a forum for dialogue has been suggested by Roberta Paikoff. She advocates creating a collaborative advisory board that includes community members, researchers, and interventionists. Another alternative is to schedule rounds of face-to-face conversations or group meetings with social scientists, client experts, and representatives of other CBOs several times a year. As an ongoing procedure, log client questions, requests, complaints, and compliments; this is the simplest form of recording expert client input.

## Collaborative Needs Assessment and Combining Expertise

There is no one right way to do a needs assessment. In fact, the right way is to use several methods at once. It is a rule of science that one study does not give a firm answer to any question. There is always a nagging feeling that the results of a study could have happened by chance or were due to special circumstances, especially if the study is very small, with few people participating. The most convincing findings come from an accumulation of evidence, especially if that evidence comes from several different sources, uses several different methodologies, and represents the work of people who are either unbiased about the issue or have very different positions about the matters at hand. (See Chapter 5 for a description of a needs assessment conducted in just such a manner.)

Social scientists, CBOs, and clients working together can be very creative in designing routine needs assessments at very low cost. When all these parties work together, the needs assessment can be incorporated into an organization's routine daily, monthly, or annual work and is not something special that requires creating a special budget line. The assessment can be designed to represent client viewpoints, CBO viewpoints, and good science all at once. By using this approach, programming proposals can grow out of identified needs that are securely grounded in the community.

For example, to get the funding I now have, my needs assessments consisted of the following:

- Sending out 10 parent volunteers on 10 consecutive days for two hours each day to interview every third adult they saw on assigned street corners with a three-minute interview script about AIDS-related community needs
- Keeping a log of questions participants asked in another project
- Borrowing and updating a guide to services on the Lower East Side from the Lower East Side AIDS Strategy Group
- Reviewing the HIV/AIDS quarterly surveillance update from the New York City Department of Health
- Acquiring a community profile update from the New York State Department of Health AIDS Institute
- Asking participants in a former project what they liked and disliked about that project
- Maintaining client attendance records to determine which services were used and which were not
- Running focus groups with children age 8 to 18 from the community about what was hard and easy about growing up in the neighborhood and who they usually went to or wanted to go to for advice

These methods were not complicated, but they were designed to answer specific questions that someone who did not know the community would want answered: Does the community want this, do they need this, and is anybody else doing it already? If we do it, is anyone likely to come? In the process, we got a surprise. We thought we wanted to design a program to help parents become HIV prevention educators of their own children. What we found out was that 1 of 10 people on the Lower East Side were already HIV-infected, and it was equally important to teach parents and children how to socialize comfortably and safely with their aunts, uncles, cousins, classmates, and family friends who are HIV-infected. This is now one of the best parts of our program—something we would not have implemented without community input.

Coover and colleagues describe an ingenious project in which a Head Start program and a local health department collaborated. They discovered that parents were very concerned about the high prevalence of asthma among their children and their children's friends. The parents thought there was nothing they could do about asthma, which they saw as a medical problem that only doctors could solve. The health department knew better, and parents were taught low-cost ways to identify and clean up environmental conditions that aggravate asthma and allergies, such as cleaning up mold and mildew, substituting plastic toys for stuffed toys, and identifying hypoallergenic pets. The program dealt with the problem in three ways: by asking a simple set of questions about the parents' concerns for their children's health, by encouraging parents to take photos of environmental conditions with project-provided cameras, and providing information from the health department about ways of preventing asthma attacks.

There are times when a needs assessment conducted by one organization can serve several organizations. For example, the information gained from the needs assessment conducted for the Head Start asthma project could also be used to stimulate similar projects in nursery and elementary schools. I have shared data with many CBOs to help them justify programs to policy makers and obtain additional funding.

Social scientists can lead brainstorming sessions with CBOs and clients to develop workable solutions to joint problems. They can use established theory to modify these solutions. There is a very old set of ideas in psychology—variously labeled *functionalism* or *social evolution*—that suggests that some community members have already found individual solutions to problems, but nobody else knows about these solutions, or perhaps these particular community members think that their situations are unique. Social scientists can use research to find and test these solutions. Then these solutions, fine-tuned with insights from social science theory, can be taught to others. It is from this kind of research that social scientists found out about the importance of parental monitoring—that is, always knowing where their kids are, what they are doing, and making sure they do important things, like homework—in preventing adolescent substance use in high-risk neighborhoods.

Donald Campbell, a famous social psychological researcher, said that if we are to understand the world, we need two kinds of people: (1) people who understand problems in depth from a particular viewpoint and (2) people who can move between and bridge several viewpoints. He called this the "fishscale" model of omniscience or knowing everything. It would look like this:

)  *Expert in area 1*
  )    *Bridge person who knows about areas 1 and 2*
)  *Expert in area 2*

If we are serious about giving back to the community, it is in our interest to begin creating Campbell's bridge people. One center for the study of HIV, for example, has a program that funds social scientists to spend 10% of their time making alliances with CBOs. They try to understand the characteristics of CBOs that make it easy or hard for them to add new programs that research has demonstrated will work. The American Psychological Association (APA) has created a list of behavioral science volunteers who will offer their expertise to community planning groups formed by the Centers for Disease Control. The goal is to assist the planning groups in implementing HIV programs in their states or cities. The APA has sent these volunteers literature and will establish other forms of training for them to learn how to work effectively with community groups. Individual projects, including my own, have encouraged clients or staff to pursue additional education in hopes of becoming heads of CBOs or social science researchers.

This mentoring and guidance can be built into a project or program. In my own research and service programs, I have established a new custom: We bring a few clients, frontline staff, and community members to research conferences, sometimes as co-presenters. I've found that this experience has profound effects: The whole research enterprise is demystified. Clients and staff are able to see the real people behind the research establishment. Participants begin to learn that their problems are not only local but also perhaps national or global. They hear their own thoughts and observations summarized by people identified as "distinguished scientists." They make alliances and meet people. They realize that there are some things they understand well (e.g., the problems of implementing HIV prevention programs in neighborhoods at risk around the world) and others not so well (e.g., data analysis). They realize that they have a lot to tell the scientists about what it feels like to be a client, what issues have been overlooked, and what has not been well explained. They want to come back, they want to do more, and they want to know more. One client participant, almost immediately on her return from a conference, embarked on a new career path, completed a GED within months of her return, and committed herself to a career in health services.

We cannot help everyone with every problem, but we can develop a client-friendly referral system. As mentioned previously, we work in a neighborhood in which HIV is highly prevalent—as are violence, poverty, and unemployment. HIV infection is not the only serious health problem associated with poverty; others include high blood pressure, diabetes, and asthma. Sometimes clients cannot read the letter they just got from welfare or have nothing to eat and nowhere to stay. One of our staff members, Edna Bula, who coordinated our field operation, convinced us to develop a referral system to offer some assistance to meet a variety of needs. We accomplished this goal, and then, every time she made a referral, she followed up by checking with the agencies and clients about the referral. Slowly she created a list of service providers who treated clients well. She also developed first-name-basis relationships with staff from an entire network of organizations and was able to let them know what clients had reported to her about their experiences.

This simple system of referral and follow-up greatly increased the neighborhood's respect for our project. We were seen as responsive, not simply as imposing our priorities. In addition, other CBOs also perceived us as helpful. Sometimes we had to reschedule our work while the client met a more urgent need, which is okay. We understood when a client needed to pick up her children from school or keep an appointment at the welfare office. Like a physician treating a patient with several problems, we learned to negotiate and communicate about what was most important to do first.

The referral system Edna developed also gave us data about clients' met and unmet needs. We will incorporate these into our next service program and in future grant proposals. Some of these

*Our research team in front of the field site. From left to right (top row): Christopher Godfrey, James Pride, Bea Krauss, Richard Velez, Durline Yee; (bottom row): Rees Davis, Joanne O'Day, Yolanda Jones, Teasha Daniels*

unmet needs, we recognize, are outside our organization's mission. We do, however, often share this data with other organizations designed to provide the needed services.

## Compensating Clients and Providing Information and Opportunities

In our experience, clients do not wish to be compensated only with money and small services that make their participation in our programs easier, such as transportation, babysitting, and meals. They also wish to be compensated with recognition, respect, and opportunity. In our program, we give parents training on how to be HIV prevention educators of their own children. We also have parents and children fill out research questionnaires and participate in research interviews. We make it very clear that we are paying parents and children for their *time,* not for their information. If we pay them for the former, we are recognizing they have other obligations and that their time is valuable. If we pay them for the latter, we are coercing them and undermining any sincere motivation parents have to prevent HIV among the youth of the community. At the end of parent training, we give out certificates of completion—a colorful signed certificate (Figure 6-1). After parents and children practice talking about HIV together, we give the parent and child a similar communication certificate. Parents and children show a genuine pride in these certificates, sometimes displaying them on the walls of their homes. Clients, like everyone else, want to be honored for their achievements as well as paid for their time. It was our parent-and-child community advisory boards who first suggested the use of certificates to us.

Likewise, during the training—which involves a lot of give and take—parents wished to have their insights and suggestions noted or recognized. An excellent trainer with whom we work suggested it is disrespectful to dismiss out of hand what clients already do to cope with the difficulties they face. It is more respectful to offer them alternatives and assist them in evaluating those alternatives. Finally, clients often expressed the desire to be compensated with additional opportunities. They want to be able to gain more

**FIGURE  6-1    Sample of Certificate**

## The Lower East Side Health Projects

*This certifies that*

_____

*regularly completed a three-hour training course*

_____

*at*

**National Development and Research Institutes**

**satellite office 97-99 Avenue B, NYC**

_____          _____
**Principal Investigator**                    **Date**

information or skills, learn what happened to the information that they had given, participate in a more active way in the project, or learn how they could perhaps find employment, as did some of our staff members from the community.

When a number of clients make a request, an organization can respond with illustrated booklets or brochures, telephone hotline numbers, instructional videos or computer software, locations of workshops, or reading lists. Such items developed by a CBO can be made generally available to the community through dissemination to other organizations and in answer to requests at your site. Although we are a research organization obligated to one project, we have given lunch hour or after-hour presentations—"An

Overview of HIV Infection," for example—to women in housing shelters, to junior high school classes, to parents and children in transitional housing (midway between homeless shelters and apartments), and to other organizations on a voluntary basis. Senior staff are often co-presenters in these situations. The community thus sees the senior staff as present in the community, and the senior staff has the opportunity to hear directly the questions and concerns of community members.

Some organizations have formalized their presentation products as a speaker's bureau or a list of available workshops. Because we collaborate with a training institute and with Cornell University's extension service, we are able to refer clients to workshops that have the potential not only to advance their skills but also to set them on career paths. We also provide written guides to local health and social service agencies. We are a family-oriented project concerned with HIV infection, uniquely able to provide every family with a guide to local HIV-related services and youth-related services. These guides are multipurpose. They serve as part of our needs assessment, part of our referral system, and, in the hands of our clients, part of our services. The more multipurpose products developed, the better served are the organization, the clients, and the community.

Because we have given presentations and developed materials that we have shared with other organizations, those organizations are willing to assist us with their expertise. Recently, for example, we heard of three children who found discarded syringes on playgrounds, and one child was stuck by a syringe. In response, the local needle exchange gave a presentation to our staff about the safe handling and discarding of syringes. With the assistance of the needle exchange and parent advisors, we were able to create a guide for parents on how to use paper or Styrofoam coffee cups to pick up syringes, how to use coffee cans or drink jars secured with lids or masking tape to carry the syringes, and which local clinics and facilities accept syringes for disposal. This illustrated guide is now included in an information packet we give to every parent.

We can also provide clients with opportunities to learn what happens to research or service information. Every researcher and service organization at some time must write a report or give a presentation about accomplishments. Some organizations produce newsletters, lists of accomplishments, or annual reports. It is relatively simple to edit these summary documents so that they are appropriate for and accessible to your client population. The findings and accomplishments can then be given to clients who request them. The requests can be gathered as part of a routine intake or follow-up. Summaries can be disseminated through mailings, annual scheduled presentations, or both. No matter what method of dissemination is chosen, it is important to include some client views of programs or services within the summary or presentation to demonstrate respect for client input.

Finally, we can offer the community the chance to participate more fully in programs or projects. Usually there are several different ways to do this. If the organization has rolling and staggered terms of service on its advisory boards (six months, one year, or two years), there are recurring opportunities for current or former clients to join. Community members may also be able to join a volunteer group associated with the project or organization. When they are carefully supervised and well run, volunteer experiences can provide the seasoning that can expand a résumé and sometimes result in jobs. It is important that volunteers abide by rules for attendance, time, and effort; have in-service training to increase their information and skills, undergo orientations that clearly define roles to prevent misunderstandings with paid staff, and learn appropriate behavior within organizations. We have had former clients and staff members return to school and join our project as social science or social service interns or for independent study in research. We were also able to negotiate with local schools to get social service credit for the members of our children's advisory board.

## Training an Organization

Take the viewpoint of a client entering the organization. Which person do clients first meet, what do they see, and what do they hear? Chances are that clients' first contacts are with auxiliary staff such as parking lot attendants, security, or reception personnel. How do they greet clients, talk on the phone to clients, guide clients, or handle client records? Do they talk about clients who are not present? Do they reassure clients who dropped in without an appointment that they will be served? Do their actions conform to the aims and goals of the research or service? Is their style of action appropriate to what the organization wants to achieve with clients and to its aims and goals? We believe that it is important to train the organization about the program or project from top to bottom, inside and out.

In services research, there is a concept called *low-threshold services,* meaning that it is easy for the client to enter services or programs. For some low-threshold programs, the doorway comes to the client, such as a medical van, a program providing home visits, or street-level services. In others, an outreach worker or buddy escorts the client through the doorway. Often, however, our barriers are interpersonal rather than physical. Staff may not understand how frightening a new or large institution is to a client, how uncomfortable a client may feel about lack of language skills, or how much easier it would be to walk away.

We have found that an excellent training technique for new staff is to pretend to be a client. The mock client develops a background and need story and then experiences the program or project from calling up for an appointment through receiving the service. This experience sharpens the staff member's notions of what the program or project can and cannot do and cogently illustrates how important every interaction is to potential clients. We have gotten some excellent suggestions from staff who have undergone this experience on how to improve our presentation to clients and how to prepare clients for procedures and experiences that they may not expect. The more challenging the staff member made the background of the mock client, the more interesting were the insights gained.

Beyond program staff, every contact person—such as the security guard, receptionist, and parking lot attendant—requires training. A client cannot be expected to discriminate between who is part of the program team and who is not. Their training may be less intense than the training of the organization's top personnel, but it is still necessary. Sometimes even well-trained staff cannot anticipate every situation that arises. An organization may have added Creole-, Mandarin-, and Spanish-speaking staff to a project, but what happens when a client speaks Polish or Urdu? Again, trades and alliances between organizations and referral sources might come into play. Several well-known New York City hospitals, for example, have developed linkages with a local college that has a multiethnic student body and a strong health education program. A college program provides translation services on call for a multitude of languages and dialects.

## Training for the Community

There are few jobs in poor communities. When a program comes into the community, clients see new people with new jobs. Often, clients feel underqualified for these jobs. We have found that it is mutually beneficial to identify jobs that may be transitional—that is, stepping stones to more advanced positions. We have advertised and conducted free workshops in the neighborhood to create a pool of people who may then be eligible for transitional employment. After hiring, more workshops are conducted, including resume writing and career assessment, to advance community members' skills and knowledge of the workplace. During our job preparation program, we employ a checklist (Figure 6-2) that helps us assess a client's progress. Some programs, such as those of Roberta Paikoff and Loretta Sweet Jemmott, have gone further than ours by making the intensive training of community members to fill important program positions part of their program protocols.

## Enacting Collaboration Daily

It is one thing to be introduced to the community, and another to be an integral part of the community—that is, demonstrating an ongoing commitment to community issues. We advocate an active and involved community advisory board that meets for regularly scheduled meetings and whenever emergencies arise. A

**FIGURE  6-2    Example: Simple Checklist for Job Preparation Program**

_____ completed GED on (date)

_____ did internship (start date to end date, organization and description of experience on file)

_____ wrote résumé (date, copy on file)

_____ three letters of recommendation on file (date, copies on file)

_____ applied for 30 jobs (start date to end date, descriptions on file)

_____ got five interviews (dates, job descriptions on file)

_____ got full-time job (starting date, organization, job description on file)

_____ retained full-time employment for one year (verification date)

community advisory board keeps an organization abreast of community issues; it can also be involved in each and every phase of research or programming. In our research project, community members review materials, methods, procedures, results, articles, and presentations and act as co-presenters at meetings. Their input is invaluable. To illustrate, our community advisors helped us deal with a very difficult research problem. We are psychologists mandated by New York State to report child abuse or neglect. We work with parents and children within families, interviewing them in depth about family life. We worried that if we ever had to report child abuse, the community would hear about it and no longer trust us enough to share their personal information with us. The community advisory board helped us word our research consent form so that our obligation was clear. We made it very specific that we were not obligated to report normal forms of parental discipline, just situations in which children were in grave danger. The advisory board also helped us revise the parent education program we developed until every single activity and exercise was understandable, engaging, and effective.

## Client-Based Evaluation

I have described how community input is important in developing new programs or projects; earlier, I wrote how community input is important in identifying needs. Clients and community members are also important in evaluating programs to see if they have the desired outcomes or effects. But there are two very important philosophical issues here: Who is the client and what is the desired outcome?

Is the client the next person who walks into the organization, the next generation, or the society at large? Defining the client for a project or program is not an easy task and deserves both careful thought from the staff and input from the community. An organization's definition of clients can become quite sophisticated and multifaceted. An organization serving several subgroups or factions can imagine the client as a combination of those subgroups or imagine different aspects of its programs serving different clients, as the lanes in a swimming pool serve adults doing laps and the free swim area serves smaller children. Staff also have needs that must be met and should be considered organizational "clients." In one public health course I taught, I decided the client was the students who would graduate and make public health decisions that potentially affected my children as they grew to adulthood. I taught that course very carefully. I served not only the students but also the college in which I taught, the future employers of the students, and current and future generations who would receive public health services from my students.

An organization that puts it all together—need, process, program, outcome—and stops every so often to ask clients, "How am I doing?" as did former New York City Mayor Ed Koch, is doing evaluation based on continuous client-centered quality improvement, as described by Bookbinder and colleagues (1996). One of the easiest forms of client-centered evaluation of process and program is to have community members, rather than staff, act as mock clients every so often and report on their experiences. They may identify different issues than those envisioned by the staff. Role reversal can also enable project evaluators to be mock staff. Why is this important? Would anyone want to stay at a hospital where the patients are very comfortable but it is difficult for the nurses to check on patients or hear their call buttons? Just as programs must be designed for clients who exist, they also must be designed for staff members who exist.

In some cases, only simple evaluation forms are required. At minimum, they should ask: How well did this program serve your needs? What parts of it were most helpful and least helpful? What would have made this program better for you? Outcomes, depending on what they are, can be more difficult or quite easy to measure. Measuring outcomes can be as easy as check marks on a checklist.

## Collaboration with Community Organizations

Collaboration can be built into projects as a technical assistance arm of the organization. In true community collaborations, several organizations build on one another's strengths in an equal partnership. Research and service organizations, for example, can write proposals, obtain funds, and design and evaluate programs together, with each organization having nearly equal roles from the outset. An executive officer of a CBO can be a co-investigator on research designed to develop and test a needed community program, for example. If less involvement is required, one organization can offer technical assistance to another free, for a fee, or as a trade for technical assistance or other services. Some of this technical assistance can be offered voluntarily, perhaps by becoming a member of a community organization's advisory board or council.

When a new organization is forming—from a group of current or former clients with similar needs, for example—a greater infusion of support and resources may be necessary. The support may be political and social as well as technical. Jana, for example, desired to prevent HIV infection among commercial sex workers in India. He knew the women depended on their trade for the survival needs of their families. He assisted them in forming cooperatives that sold safer sex products and in removing themselves from the financial control of landlords, moneylenders, and the organizers of the sex trade.

## CONCLUSION

In ending this chapter, I would like to note a growing positive trend. More and more, researchers are being asked to leave in place, after the evaluation is completed, the programs they began. Discussing this issue in depth is beyond the scope of this chapter. However, such an undertaking would require collaboration with the community from the outset, perhaps including training of "bridge" people to conduct ongoing needs assessment and client-centered evaluation to ensure that the program remains faithful to its aims. Such a transfer would also assume that technical assistance will be available as needed and that necessary resources will be made available as the program is handed over to the community. Perhaps such a plan will represent the ultimate in fair interchange. The clients, service providers, and researchers would become colleagues.

## SUGGESTED READINGS

Altman, D. G. (1995). Sustaining interventions in community systems: On the relationship between researcher and communities. *Health Psychology, 14,* 526–536.

Bookbinder, M., Coyle, N., Kiss, M., Goldstein, M., Holritz, K., Thaler, H., Gianella, A., Derby, S., Brown, M., Racolin, A.,

Ho, M. N., & Portenoy, R. K. (1996). Implementing national standards for cancer pain management: Program model and evaluation. *Journal of Pain and Symptom Management, 12,* 334–347.

Bracht, N., Finnegan, J. R., Rissel, C., Weisbrod, R., Gleason, J., Corbett, J., & Veblen-Mortenson, S. (1994). Community ownership and program continuation following a health demonstration project. *Health Education Research: Theory and Practice, 9,* 243–255.

Gamble, V. N. (1993). A legacy of distrust: African Americans and medical research. *American Journal of Preventive Medicine, 9,* 35–38.

Hawe, P., Noort, M., King, L., & Jordens, C. (1997). Multiplying health gains: The critical role of capacity-building within health promotion programs. *Health Policy, 39,* 29–42.

Kalichman, S. (1998). *Understanding AIDS.* Washington, DC: American Psychological Association.

Krauss, B., Goldsamt, L., Bula, E., & Sember, R. (1997). The white researcher in the multicultural community: Lessons in HIV prevention education learned in the field. *Journal of Health Education, 28,* 67–71.

Steckler, A., & Goodman, R. M. (1989). How to institutionalize health promotion programs. *American Journal of Health Promotion, 3,* 34–44.

Steinbarger, B., & Smith, H. (1996). Assessing the quality of counseling services: Developing accountable helping systems. *Journal of Counseling and Development, 75,* 145–148.

Thomas, S. B., & Quinn, S. C. (1991). The Tuskegee syphilis study, 1932 to 1972: Implications for HIV education and AIDS risk education programs in the black community. *American Journal of Public Health, 81,* 1498–1505.

# 7

# PROTECTING PARTICIPANTS IN FIELD-BASED PROJECTS

**SHERRY DEREN, PH.D., and JOHN BAUMANN, PH.D.**

Protecting the rights of clients or research subjects who are the focus of field-based projects is a concern to be addressed in all aspects of project development, implementation, management, and evaluation. Doing so is necessary to meet both ethical mandates and legal requirements. Particular challenges arise with field-based projects, where the application of policies and procedures, often developed for institution-based settings, may be difficult. Although projects that are primarily service or research in orientation may have different specific concerns, general issues of inclusion, informed consent, and privacy and confidentiality are relevant to both. The purpose of this chapter is to provide a summary of the regulations and an introduction to the institutions that help to ensure the ethical treatment of research participants and service clients. To demonstrate the practical application of some of these rules and laws, the boxed inserts throughout the chapter describe some of the ethical dilemmas that we have faced as researchers in the field, along with their resolutions. Every project faces its own unique problems, but we hope that the principles laid out in this chapter will be helpful in developing solutions to address them.

Many field-based projects, regardless of whether they have primarily a service or research orientation, address marginalized and stigmatized populations—for example, ethnic minorities, injection drug users, and the homeless. These groups have sometimes found that their rights as consumers of services, as citizens, or as research subjects have not been fully considered, and clarification of these rights for both staff and clients is an important part of field project activities. This chapter addresses the most important rights as an introduction to many of the issues relating to participants' rights that may arise in conducting field research. Its contents cannot substitute for administrative, legal, or local IRB (institutional review board) review of projects, however. In addition, local regulations regarding reporting requirements, if applicable, must be followed.

The following sections provide an overview of the legislation and policies regarding the rights of participants in service and research projects, followed by more detailed discussion of the key issues of risks and benefits, fairness of inclusion, informed consent, and confidentiality as they apply to field-based service and research projects.

Prior to such a discussion, however, it may be useful to clarify several terms. For the purposes of this chapter, *research* refers to those activities

> designed to test an hypothesis, permit conclusions to be drawn, and thereby to develop or contribute to generalizable knowledge (expressed, for example, in theories, principles, and statements of relationships). Research is usually described in a formal protocol that sets forth an objective and a set of procedures designed to reach that objective. (NIH, Belmont report)

*Service* refers to

> interventions that are designed solely to enhance the wellbeing of an individual patient or client that have a reason-

able expectation of success. The purpose of medical or behavioral [service] practice is to provide diagnosis, preventive treatment or therapy to particular individuals. (NIH, Belmont Report)

Even though much of what we say here pertains to both service and research projects, the regulations governing these two areas are often derived from different sources.

## INSTITUTIONALIZATION OF PROTECTIONS

Despite a historical record that contains dramatic examples of violations of the rights and protections of human participants, we must also recognize that protections have been, to varying degrees, institutionalized in the practice of research and social service delivery. Dating as far back as the Hippocratic Oath of "do no harm," professional associations of practitioners and researchers, individual service and research organizations, and funding sources have each developed codes of ethics that prescribe how their respective clients and subjects ought to be treated. Moreover, various local, state, and federal government agencies have similarly issued and enforced guidelines for the conduct of service delivery and research.

### Regulations Protecting Research Participants

The National Commission for the Protection of Human Subjects in Biomedical and Behavioral Research was created in July 1974 to identify ethical principles and develop guidelines for biomedical and behavioral research. These principles and guidelines were formally released in 1979. Strictly speaking, these guidelines are applicable only to federally funded research projects, but they have rapidly become the gold standard for research funded through private foundations and by other means and are generally followed today. The three principles that underlie the conduct of research are respect for persons, beneficence, and justice (Table 7-1).

**TABLE 7-1    Principles Underlying the Conduct of Research**

- *Respect for Persons*: "Respect for persons incorporates at least two basic ethical convictions: first that individuals should be treated as autonomous agents, and second, that persons with diminished autonomy are entitled to protection. The principle of respect for persons thus divides into two separate moral requirements: the requirement to acknowledge autonomy and the requirement to protect those with diminished autonomy." (Belmont Report: 4–5)
- *Beneficence*: "Persons are treated in an ethical manner not only by respecting their decisions and protecting them from harm, but also by making efforts to secure their well-being. Such treatment falls under the principle of beneficence. The term 'beneficence' is often understood to cover acts of kindness or charity that go beyond strict obligation. In this document, beneficence is understood in a stronger sense: (1) do not harm and (2) maximize possible benefits and minimize possible harms." (Belmont Report: 6)
- *Justice*: "Who ought to receive the benefits of research and bear its burdens? This is a question of justice, in the sense of 'fairness in distribution' or 'what is deserved.' An injustice occurs when some benefit to which a person is entitled is denied without good reason or when some burden is imposed unduly." (Belmont Report: 8)

The procedural guidelines used to implement these principles are informed consent, assessment of risks and benefits, and selection of subjects. These procedures are described in Table 7-2. These principles and regulations have been codified by the federal government as Title 45, Part 46 of the Code of Federal Regulations (45 CFR 46). Within the Department of Health and Human Services, the Office for Protection from Research Risks (OPRR) was formed. In June 2000, OPRR was reorganized as the Office of Human Research Protections to oversee the implementation and enforcement of these regulations, as well as to provide "guidance on ethical issues in biomedical or behavioral research."

**TABLE 7-2   Procedural Guidelines for**
            **Implementing Research Principles**

- *Informed Consent*: "Respect for persons requires that subjects, to the degree that they are capable, be given the opportunity to choose what shall or shall not happen to them. This opportunity is provided when adequate standards for informed consent are satisfied." (Belmont Report: 10)
- *Assessment of Risks and Benefits*: "The assessment of risks and benefits requires a careful array of relevant data, including, in some cases, alternative ways of obtaining the benefits sought in the research. Thus, the assessment presents both an opportunity and a responsibility to gather systematic and comprehensive information about proposed research. For the investigator, it is a means to examine whether the proposed research is properly designed. For a review committee, it is a method for determining whether the risks that will be presented to subjects are justified. For prospective subjects, the assessment will assist the determination whether or not to participate." (Belmont Report: 14–15)
- *Selection of Subjects*: "Just as the principle of respect for persons finds expression in the requirements for consent, and the principle of beneficence in risk/benefit assessment, the principle of justice gives rise to moral requirements that there be fair procedures and outcomes in the selection of research subjects." (Belmont Report: 18)

## Regulations Protecting Recipients of Services

The regulations related to the delivery of medical and social services are more diverse and subject to the jurisdiction of more agencies. For instance, federal, state, and local governments have each enacted important and enforceable regulations that affect the work of the service provider and the delivery of services.

The major categories of protections discussed in this chapter are confidentiality and informed consent. The concerns over confidentiality apply to such issues as HIV status, alcohol and drug abuse patient records, and mental health status. For instance, at the federal level, one of the most important codifications of these protections is Confidentiality of Alcohol and Drug Abuse Patient Records: 42 CFR 2. An example at the state level is New York State Public Health Law, Article 27-F: HIV and AIDS Related Information, which outlines the requirements of informed consent and confidentiality with regard to HIV testing.

The standards developed for the protection of clients' HIV status, alcohol and drug abuse, and mental health records are equally applicable to information concerning such matters as criminality, sexual orientation, employment status, and income. Regulations also state the responsibility of service providers to obtain informed consent from consumers of their services. The guidelines or regulations regarding other issues discussed later, such as inclusion and risk/benefit ratio, are generally less systematically institutionalized or formally articulated. They may, however, be covered by more general laws or regulations prohibiting discrimination, malpractice, or negligence.

Throughout this chapter, we refer to the principles, guidelines, and regulations developed and enforced by the federal government and/or the state of New York, which are our point of reference for two reasons: (1) the standards are frequently used as models for other authorities and (2) they are frequently among the most stringent and most protective. State requirements are generally more stringent than federal rules.

## KEY ISSUES

### Risks and Benefits

Risks to individuals participating in service or research projects should be justified by the anticipated benefits provided by that project. This justification, often called the risk/benefit ratio, relates to the principles of respect for persons and beneficence, as described in Table 7-1. Project staff should be sensitive to risks of either physical or psychological harm at all stages of project development and implementation.

**Release of Information**

One day, a policeman called our community-based research site and was quite upset. During an arrest, he had been pricked with a needle belonging to a suspect who was also one of our participants. The policeman wanted to know the client's HIV status. Normally, this request would have been rebuffed without question. The federal certificate of confidentiality that protects our research allows us not to have to divulge any information regarding our participants. In this case, however, the subject asked that our HIV counselor share his results with the policeman. He had given the policeman our address and telephone number to contact us for his results because the person had been tested several months ago by our staff and signed a consent form to release HIV-related information. We consulted with our attorney and compared the participant's signature on the release-of-information form with the original consent forms on file. To the best of our ability, we made sure that the client was not coerced or bullied in any way and that, in fact, it could be beneficial to him to meet his request to reveal his results. His HIV test results, including the date of testing, were revealed to the policeman.

To protect participants from harm, activities must be carried out by appropriately trained and licensed staff (e.g., nurses, HIV counselors). A program of continual staff training and supervision (as described in Chapter 4) is also needed to ensure that a high performance level is maintained. Project staff also must ensure that the setting for the conduct of research or provision of services is appropriately designed. For instance, the health needs of the staff and clients may require special equipment for ventilation or sterilization, or the physical environment may need to be altered or renovated to provide privacy and confidentiality. In addition, individuals involved in a project may not be unfairly deprived of recommended treatments that are available, as occurred with the Tuskegee syphilis study or has been of concern in terms of the availability of HIV/AIDS medications to all who are eligible and can benefit.

The issue of risks and benefits has been most fully articulated with regard to the conduct of research projects. Beyond the general principles incorporated in the codes of ethics of the various professional associations, there does not appear to be a coherent set of standards regarding the application of risk/benefit considerations to the provision of social or medical services or health-related interventions. These services may be subject to a variety of laws or regulations, such as those governing negligence or malpractice. Therefore, projects should consult with an attorney, state official, or representative of a professional association regarding the laws and regulations of their particular location and professional association.

All codes of research ethics are based on the principle that any risks to research participants must be justified by anticipated benefits. Ensuring this requirement is a major responsibility of institutional review boards (IRBs). *Risk* is defined as "the probability of harm or injury (physical, psychological, social, or economic) occurring as a result of participation in a research study" (OPRR 1993, G–12). *Benefit* is defined as "a valued or desired outcome; an advantage" (OPRR 1993, G–1). Benefits of research fall into two major categories: benefits to subjects and benefits to society. Frequently, research may have no immediate benefit to the research participants, but the findings may result in benefits to society. For example, studies of new treatments for disease, including medications, may require providing placebo treatments to some participants. Although these individuals will not benefit from this treatment, the findings of the study may make more effective treatments available to everyone. Note that payments to subjects for participating in research may not be considered as "benefits" from the research.

As prescribed by federal regulation (45 CFR 46), an organization's institutional review board is required to assess whether the research presents greater than minimal risk. If minimal risk exists, under certain conditions, the IRB may be allowed to pro-

---

### Violating Confidentiality: "Requirement to Report"

During a counseling session, a client revealed that she thought she had killed someone during one of her drinking binges. Although she thought that she might have had a hallucination, she was pretty sure that the incident had actually happened. The counselor was concerned about the project's obligations to notify proper authorities and reported it to her project director, who promptly spoke to the principal investigator. Once all available information was collected from the project staff, a representative of our institutional review board was contacted. Because of the unique circumstances, we agreed that we should seek the guidance of an official from the Office for Protection from Research Risk (OPRR). Interestingly, we discovered that there is no hard-and-fast rule; the obligation to report varies from state to state, depending on state laws. If the project is operating in a state that has enacted a "requirement to report" ruling for crimes of which a citizen becomes aware, then the organization must break confidentiality. If the state has no such requirement, the organization is not permitted to break confidentiality. The same situation is true regarding other issues, such as HIV status, AIDS, other sexually transmitted diseases, and illegal behavior.

---

vide expedited review of proposals. A waiver or modification of consent requirements may also be permitted. In research presenting more than minimal risks, a more elaborate procedure is required to ensure that subjects are fully informed of the risks and benefits, of the availability of alternative treatment, and that they may be compensated in the case of research-related injuries.

The major ethical judgment made by an IRB is evaluation of the risk/benefit ratio. Steps include (1) the identification of the risks, (2) determination of the severity of the risk, (3) identification of probable benefits, (4) determination that the risks are reasonable in relation to the benefits, (5) assurance that potential subjects are provided with an accurate description of the risks and anticipated benefits, and (6) determination of intervals of periodic review. Different IRBs may arrive at different assessments, because judgments often depend on prevailing community standards and the subjective determinations of IRB members. All IRBs, in addition, are subject to institutional constraints, federal regulations, and state law.

## Fairness of Inclusion

The issue of fairness of inclusion relates to (1) the distribution of the services to be provided, (2) the generalizability of the knowledge to be generated, and (3) the distribution of the burdens of the research to be conducted. It also requires that people are treated equally. The principle of fairness of inclusion, therefore, relates to matters of both inclusion in and exclusion from participation in programs of research and service. Methods to determine who will receive services or who will be recruited for research must be examined to assess whether particular groups of individuals, such as minorities or women, are being unfairly excluded or included.

Federal research regulations currently require scrutiny regarding inclusion of women, minorities, and children. The principal investigator has the responsibility to either representatively include these parties or provide a justification for the systematic exclusion of any group. Thus, selection of subjects must be equitable, to help ensure that the burdens and benefits of research are fairly distributed.

This fairness doctrine is also important in terms of how well the research findings can be generalized across populations. For example, early research regarding prevention of heart attacks focused primarily on male populations, and the generalizability of findings to women was questionable. This area of study, as well as others in which women were systematically excluded, contributed to the establishment of the Office of Research on Women's Health at the National Institutes on Health (NIH) to ensure, among other mandates, that women are included as participants in NIH-supported research.

With regard to the provision of social services, the fairness doc-trine has generally been defined and enforced in reference to the prohibition of discrimination. Program staff need to ensure that their services are provided across population groups to all who are eligible, without prejudice. Types of discrimination prohibited extend beyond race, ethnicity, gender, and sexual orientation to include issues of poverty and access to resources. For example, public hospitals in New York City are required to provide services regardless of patients' ability to pay.

## Informed Consent

Emanating from the principle of respect for persons, informed con-sent procedures have been developed to provide individuals with the opportunity to decide what will or will not happen to them. Central themes of informed consent include information, compre-hension, and the voluntary nature of participation. Compliance requires providing information to participants, ensuring that they understand this information, and seeing that their consent is given voluntarily and free of coercion or undue influence. An example of coercion is threatening the loss of other services if the individual chooses not to participate. Undue influence may occur through an offer of excessive or improper reward to obtain compliance.

Informed consent requirements for participants in research projects that have been developed provide for eight basic elements: (1) a description of the study and procedures; (2) a description of any foreseeable risks or benefits; (3) a disclosure of alternative courses of treatment; (4) an explanation of the extent to which con-fidentiality of records will be maintained; (5) an explanation of compensation; (6) for research involving more than minimal risk, information regarding treatments available; (7) information as to whom to contact for answers to questions about the research and research subjects' rights and whom to contact in the event of a research-related injury; and (8) a statement that participation is voluntary, with refusal involving no penalty or loss of benefits. Depending on the type of research, other elements may also be required. Informed consent generally consists of two documents: (1) an informed consent information sheet that provides an elaborate description of the proposed research, including the elements just discussed, and that is kept by the research subject; and (2) an informed consent signature sheet that summarizes the material on the information sheet and requires the signature of the research subject. The signature sheet is kept by the project staff in a secure location separate from any individual research data, and it becomes part of the project's documentation. Informed consent in general must be documented with written consent, and all procedures and forms must be reviewed by an IRB. In specific cases, depending on the content of the research, the research design, or the location where the research is conducted, an IRB may waive requirements for an investigator to obtain signed consent forms. Additional protections exist for research conducted with children and mentally ill individuals, as well as for prisoners and other institutionalized populations.

Although the elements of informed consent are clear, they may not be easy to achieve. For example, recruitment of active drug users for research projects may require obtaining informed consent from individuals under the influence of mind-altering substances. Training interviewers to obtain consent under these circumstances, which may involve asking the subject to return later when they may be better able to provide consent (as well as engage in the interview or the services offered), is essential to ensure adequate implementation.

In the service realm, the legal mandates for consent are generally not as clear. If research is incorporated into the service provision, the same principles of informed consent apply. In some cases, the voluntary request for services may constitute an implicit manifestation of informed consent: Informed consent is assumed when a person appears for and becomes the recipient of the service. In many cases, however, it is appropriate to obtain written informed consent as well. For many services, written informed consent is mandated by state law or regulations, institutional policy or guidelines, professional codes of behavior, or insurance regulations. For instance, individuals requesting medical treatment or

HIV testing in a community-based clinic should be, and frequently are, required to complete a written informed consent document. For complicated medical interventions, these forms can be lengthy and sometimes confusing. In these cases, enough staff time must be allotted to explain these forms and the procedures to which they refer.

In New York state, HIV testing presents a special set of circumstances for informed consent. New York requires that written informed consent and pretest and post-test counseling are part of HIV testing procedures, and the specific content of each is described in the state's public health law (Article 27-F, Section 2781: HIV and AIDS Related Information). Although the specific language and requirements for HIV testing vary from state to state, to maintain the highest standards, the informed consent documents should conform to the rigorous guidelines for HIV testing in New York and those developed for participants in federally funded research projects.

## Privacy and Confidentiality

Privacy pertains primarily to the conditions under which information is obtained, and confidentiality pertains to methods used to ensure that information about individuals is not improperly divulged. Both may present challenges in field settings. Hard-to-reach or stigmatized individuals often come to field-based projects or services under emotional strain and vulnerability, and the protection of their confidentiality, even if they do not immediately recognize its importance, should be of utmost importance to the project's staff. During the course of obtaining the information necessary to deliver appropriate services or completing a research interview instrument, the client may reveal information that must be considered highly confidential. It can be answers to questions regarding personal behaviors, such as sexual risk information obtained during HIV pretest counseling, or to questions regarding criminal or drug use behaviors. Both service and research projects must take all steps possible to guard the participant's privacy and confidentiality. In addition to the importance of confidentiality as part of the respect for persons principle, clear emphasis on the importance of confidentiality in a field site (which is quickly communicated to and sensed by clients) helps to ensure that clients provide accurate information and that they are more likely to return for follow-up or additional services.

Concerns about privacy begin with data collection. Interviews should be conducted in private offices that are soundproof. When research interviews are conducted in such unusual locations as "on the streets" or away from research field offices, private locations (e.g., an out-of-the-way booth in a coffee shop) should be sought whenever possible. As discussed in other chapters, an important part of field staff training regards client confidentiality. Information about clients should be shared with other staff only when necessary and never in public areas (e.g., client waiting rooms).

Methods for maintaining confidentiality of client information are generally required to be described in detail as part of a research grant proposal and for IRB approval (e.g., see 45 CFR 46, NIH Grants Policy Statement, and NIH grant application kit). These methods usually include the following practices: clients' names only appear on the informed consent forms, and interviews are identified only by a code number. Consent forms and interviews are stored separately (so data cannot be identified by subjects), and

---

### Violating Confidentiality: Medical Emergency

A study participant passed out at our field site, and the police and an ambulance had to be called. At the time, many other study participants were waiting for counseling sessions, interviews, and other project business at the field site. The field site manager, knowing that many of our clients are not comfortable with the police (some, in fact, may be at risk of arrest), took all the clients in the waiting room, put them in another room, and closed the door so that the police would not see them while they were tending to the unconscious person. The man was revived and given the medical attention he needed.

data forms are brought from field sites to central research facilities, where more extensive security measures are usually available, as soon as possible. Maintaining the confidentiality of information must be a consideration throughout the research process, even in the transport of data. Thus, transporting the consent forms and the interview data forms at different times, or by different staff members, helps to assure that even if one set of forms is lost, no information identifiable by person will be revealed. Storage of information that contains names should be in locked files, with keys available only to those authorized by the principal investigator. Finally, in reporting research results, information should be provided in aggregate form or, if individual quotes, vignettes, or other individual-based information is necessary for conveying the results, personal identifiers should be removed or camouflaged.

Many research projects, particularly those obtaining information regarding illegal activities, obtain a certificate of confidentiality from the Department of Health and Human Services once their data collection instruments have been developed. The certificate of confidentiality prevents the researcher from having to reveal the participation of any individual in the project. Any data collected cannot be subpoenaed or otherwise made available to legal authorities. For many researchers, informing subjects about the certificate of confidentiality, both by including it in the informed consent and referring to it when particularly sensitive information is requested, assures the subjects that the data provided cannot generally be used against them in the legal system.

Equally explicit laws or policies exist for the protection of confidentiality in service projects. At the federal level, 42 CFR 2 was enacted both to strengthen the right to privacy afforded patients in treatment and to enhance the appeal of substance abuse treatment. It identifies the rules and regulations regarding confidentiality of drug and alcohol patient records, applies broadly to all federally assisted programs, and represents the minimum that states must adopt. It specifies how information about patients is to be managed, stored, and protected; it also provides specific guidelines that have to be met prior to the release of such protected information. The overall thrust of this regulation and of related state laws is to prevent the arbitrary or unauthorized release of a wide range of treatment information about a patient or client, including:

- Application for services
- Diagnosis
- Prognosis
- Past or current treatment
- Physical whereabouts
- Status in treatment
- Attendance in treatment
- Identifying data or characteristics
- Termination from treatment
- Communications between patient and treatment staff

The only bases for disclosure are as follows:

- Written consent from the client
- Internal communications within the treatment program
- Anonymous information that is aggregated or released without identifying information
- Medical emergency
- Court order
- Crime at program or against program personnel
- Audit and/or research purposes
- Qualified service organization agreement
- Child abuse

On the local level, there may be other privacy and confidentiality regulations (e.g., New York laws regarding HIV/AIDS-related information) that may prohibit disclosure of confidential information except under very clearly and narrowly defined circumstances. In practice, many service providers have recognized that almost all violations of client privacy and confidentiality occur by accident. Many agencies conduct ongoing in-service training to review policies that protect client confidentiality, and hospitals and other large service providers now routinely post signs in elevators warning staff against discussing specific patients in such public settings.

In certain circumstances, researchers or service providers may be required or feel obligated to share confidential information. For example, they may become aware of ongoing child abuse, or participants may reveal an intent to harm themselves or others. If, by the nature of the research or service activities, the organization believes that this type of information is likely to be elicited during an interview, it is important to include this obligation as part of

---

### Confidentiality After a Participant Has Passed Away

On one of the projects we supervised, our field site manager received a call from the police regarding an unidentified dead body. When the body was found, the only identifying information that could be recovered was an appointment card from our project, with the field site telephone number. The detective assigned to the case, following the only lead he had, called the number on the card to try to identify the next of kin. The field site manager looked through the project's records and found a form with the name and telephone number of a daughter. Our project faced a serious dilemma: On the one hand, we had an obligation to protect the confidentiality of the information collected from the client, as we had promised her when she signed the consent form; on the other hand, the police told us that if she could not be identified and no family could be found, she would be buried in an unmarked grave in a potter's field. The field supervisor called the project's principal investigator, who discussed the situation with our lawyer and the secretary of the institutional review board. It was important and legally necessary to consult with both. It was finally decided that we would release the information because it posed no threat of harm to the client and, in fact, there was the potential benefit of a family-arranged funeral. The police informed the daughter of her mother's death, and the family was able to have the choice to give her a proper burial.

the informed consent. That is, the research participant should be told that staff members who learn of child abuse or of a participant's intent to harm someone may be legally and/or professionally obligated to report this information to the relevant authorities.

## CONCLUSION

The development of clear policies for staff regarding human subject issues is an initial step in addressing these concerns. Staff training that includes a review of the policies, the rationale for the development of these policies, and periodic training refreshers is also needed. Research projects are often required to undergo periodic reviews by their IRBs, whenever changes in design are contemplated, and on at least an annual basis. It is desirable for all types of community-based projects, research or service, to periodically review their procedures for safeguarding the rights of their clients and to revise their procedures as necessary.

Issues regarding the protection of human subjects arise during the course of most research and service projects. Therefore, it is important to keep lines of communication open between project staff and management, so that any concerns are reported promptly for discussion and development of corrective or preventive steps. Principal investigators of research projects are required to report any potential harm to subjects to their IRB as soon as possible. In addition, as part of their annual IRB review, they must attest that no unanticipated (or previously unreported) harm occurred to subjects since the last review. In service projects as well, any potential harm to subjects should be immediately reported to senior management. In larger institutions, reporting can usually be done through a specifically identified division, such as the office of risk management. In smaller organizations, it can be accomplished through regular meetings. For any type of project, a formal report of any incident or concern about potential harm should be prepared, including information as to (1) what occurred; (2) what redress, if any, was made; and (3) what steps have been taken (e.g., staff training or relocating confidential files) to assure that there is no recurrence.

## SUGGESTED READINGS

National Commission for the Protection of Human Subjects of Biomedical and Behavioral Research. (1979). *The Belmont Report: Ethical principles and guidelines for the protection of human subjects research.* Washington, DC: U.S. Government Printing Office.

Office for Protection from Research Risks. (1993). *Protecting human research subjects: Institutional Review Board Guidebook.* Washington, DC.

# 8

# INTEGRATING SERVICE PROVISION AND RESEARCH IN A SINGLE SETTING

## LLOYD A. GOLDSAMT, PH.D.

The overlap of research and service activities is poorly understood, largely because researchers and service providers rarely work side by side, are often antagonistic toward each other, are trained in different methodologies, and are seldom engaged in both activities. Yet, if we look closely at the daily activities of the active researcher and the active service provider, we find that both collect and evaluate information from individuals or groups and then translate that information into recommendations at the individual or societal level. Very often there is a difference in scale, in that service providers seek to rapidly use the information they gather to treat individuals in their offices, whereas researchers tend to aggregate information over a large number of individuals to make broader recommendations for treatment or prevention. Nevertheless, the fundamental tasks of both researchers and service providers are to accurately gather and interpret information for the purpose of intervening with individuals and/or large population groups.

The information researchers or service providers gather may take the form of answers to questions in an interview, responses to a written questionnaire, results of a physical examination, or results from biological testing. Although a participant may report the medications he or she is taking, as well as the illicit drugs that he or she uses, as part of a research protocol, this information is also essential for the clinical management of the participant's medical conditions. Similarly, both biological reports and self-reports of a participant's current drug use are important clinical measures, but they are also useful outcome measures in substance abuse intervention studies carried out by researchers.

Once information is collected, both researchers and service providers communicate this information directly to the patient or the research participant, other treatment professionals, insurance companies, employers, and other third parties with the patient's or participant's written consent. Certain types of medical information, such as the results of HIV tests, are reported to public health officials or to the Centers for Disease Control and Prevention. Case summaries are reported to other treatment professionals or to other members of the research team. Both researchers and service providers have developed expertise in this type of communication, and complicated treatment information or research data are presented in a clear manner, which minimizes the likelihood of confusion or misinterpretation.

With these similarities in mind, let us turn to the reasons for collaboration between researchers and service providers. For the remainder of this chapter, *research activities* refers to the subset of social science research that seeks to explain the causes and consequences of human behavior. Typically, the variables of interest are some type of observable human functioning (e.g., drug use, sexual risk taking, marital conflict, or depression) or its consequences (e.g., infection, overdose). *Services* refers to the prevention or treatment of some type of potentially harmful human behavior (e.g., methadone treatment for opiate users, public health interventions to prevent or treat disease, counseling to treat mental health and substance abuse, or medical intervention for physical or mental illness).

## WHY COMBINE RESEARCH
## AND SERVICE ACTIVITIES?

Probably the most pragmatic reason for combining service and research activities is funding. Funding for service provision is increasingly requiring research activities, usually in the form of program or service evaluation. Likewise, funding for research projects is beginning to require the inclusion of some type of service impact, either developing an intervention or disseminating research findings to frontline providers.

Research funding has traditionally been awarded on the basis of scientific methodology, potential utility of results, and feasibility of completing the work. More recently, however, funding agencies have been looking at issues of clinical applicability and dissemination of findings in their funding decisions. The federal government provides the majority of research funding in the United States. Over the years, government funding agencies have noted the tendencies of many academic researchers to disseminate their findings via academic journals. Unfortunately, the primary audience for these journals is other academic researchers and rarely frontline service providers (the medical community is sometimes an exception in this regard). Because clinical or societal relevance and necessity are important criteria in deciding which research is funded, government funding agencies have started to incorporate an applicant's plans to disseminate research into the guidelines for the funding of research grants. At my agency, we receive the majority of our funding from federal agencies. We disseminate our research findings through our training institute, which provides courses to local service providers in a variety of fields (criminal justice, substance abuse, mental health, education). The ability to disseminate our information in this fashion keeps us focused on the clinical applications of our work, provides a forum for us to interact with frontline service providers, and improves our chances of securing funds for our research projects.

Funding for service or prevention work, which typically comes from federal, state, or local government agencies or from charitable organizations, has begun to require more sophisticated evaluations of program impact. Formula funding, in which an organization would receive continued funding from the government each year based on the government's annual budget, has been the norm in some areas of prevention for decades. These funds are slowly being replaced by more competitive funding awards, in which organizations are encouraged to apply for funding for specific programs. These competitive funding mechanisms have increasingly begun to include the quality of the program evaluation in their criteria.

Earlier chapters in this book have described many situations in which research and service activities have been integrated. In Chapter 6, Bea Krauss describes conducting research with families in an inner-city, high HIV seroprevalence community, where she has addressed the service needs of a research population. Chapter 1, by Bruce Stepherson describes how to engage and work with street-based drug users. Although the activities described focus on outreach as service provision, many of the same strategies are used by researchers in working with street-based populations. In their case study (Chapter 5), Michael Clatts and colleagues describe the use of research techniques to improve the services delivered to street youth. The chapters on interviewing, conducting follow-up, and supervising staff contain material that is applicable to both research and service populations.

The preceding paragraphs have presented a rationale for integrating research and service activities. The remainder of this chapter focuses on the practical issues of this integration with hard-to-reach populations. Although much of this integration is made possible by facilitating the interaction of researchers and service providers, practical issues that vary from setting to setting must be addressed. Building on examples from earlier chapters, as well as on other National Development and Research Institutes (NDRI) projects not represented in this book, I will illustrate how projects working with stigmatized or hard-to-reach populations have addressed these practical issues, the problems that have arisen in integrating research and service activities with these populations, and how these projects have resolved these problems. Table 8-1 presents settings in which these activities can be integrated.

**TABLE  8-1    Settings in Which to Integrate
Research and Service Activities**

| *RESEARCH SETTINGS* |
| --- |
| Field offices |
| Streets (with outreach teams) |

| *SERVICE SETTINGS* |
| --- |
| Methadone programs |
| Drug treatment programs |
| Needle exchange programs |
| Homeless shelters |
| Food pantries |
| Medical clinics |
| Prisons/jails |
| Mobile outreach vans |

## INTEGRATING RESEARCH AND SERVICE ACTIVITIES

Social science research derives its relevance from its ability to understand and/or influence human behavior in a way that reflects the population of interest and is ultimately applicable to a population's needs. Whether developing a new program or collaborating on existing programs, the most important task is to have researchers and service providers consult among themselves on all aspects of the project, from program and instrument design to client care. Table 8-2 illustrates the types of service activities in which researchers can participate and the types of research activities in which service providers can participate.

Researchers can provide more clinically useful information if they have some involvement in, and understanding of, the context in which the information is collected and used. For example, when developing research protocols, researchers can attend case conferences, review client records, or pilot test interviews on actual clients. In this way, understanding the service applications of research can improve the quality and relevance of the research.

Service providers can help researchers develop real-world research questions that are applicable to the populations with whom they interact and to the institutions that serve these populations. Researchers and service providers can then work together to develop appropriate protocols to study and serve these populations.

Just as researchers benefit from understanding how their data will be used, service providers provide better research data if they understand how these data are collected, analyzed, and reported. To this end, service providers can be involved in both the collection of data and the research activities that follow data collection. For example, researchers have long known that research

**TABLE  8-2    Service Activities for Researchers and Research Activities for Service Providers**

*SERVICE ACTIVITIES FOR RESEARCHERS*

1. Serve as a "mock client" to better understand how services are provided.
2. Review a clinical chart.
3. Conduct an intake for a new client.
4. Sit in on a clinical interview.
5. Co-lead an intervention group.
6. Provide a workshop for staff, clients, and the community.
7. Give a presentation at a service-oriented conference with a provider.
8. Serve on the advisory board of a service organization.

*RESEARCH ACTIVITIES FOR SERVICE PROVIDERS*

1. Participate in the research protocol by serving as a "mock participant."
2. Code some research data.
3. Enter the research data you have coded.
4. Present data to your own treatment or prevention staff.
5. Review some research studies on the population with which you are working.
6. Present data with a researcher at a conference.
7. Serve on a community advisory board for a research project.

interviewers' participation in data entry improves the quality of the data they collect. Service providers who are given an opportunity to enter the data they collect, or allowed to assist in developing the methodology for translating their work into research data, understand how the data are ultimately used for research purposes. Ideally, researchers and service providers can together author papers, present at conferences, and conduct training.

Although researchers and service providers can benefit from close collaboration, their activities must remain separate in the eyes of participants. Ethical standards require that research participation is free of coercion and that there is no penalty for withdrawal from a research study at any time. Thus, not only must there be no *actual* connection between research participation and receipt of services but also research participants must never even *perceive* that their access to care depends on participation in a research protocol. This separation can be achieved by informing participants that certain activities are being conducted as part of their research participation, by having separate locations for service provision and research activities (e.g., separate offices in a suite of offices, separate floors of a building, or separate facilities altogether), or by having separate research and service frontline staff.

Our research projects address these issues in two different ways. To carry out research activities, some projects rent storefront space in the communities in which we work. Outreach workers then recruit participants on the streets or accept referrals from local service programs, but they carry out all of the project activities in the storefront. Other projects form alliances directly with service providers and carry out research activities in designated spaces at these service facilities. For example, NDRI research projects are currently collecting data in a local methadone clinic, a drop-in center for street youth, in school programs for at-risk youth, and in local jails and prisons. As long as the distinction between research and service activities is maintained, research and service provision can be successfully integrated in these settings.

## PROVIDING SERVICES IN RESEARCH SETTINGS

Research settings often provide ideal environments for service provision. Many researchers have gained access to the hard-to-reach populations described in this book, such as drug users, sex workers, and other marginalized groups. These groups are often underserved and frequently reluctant to engage in formal treatment. Although these populations were formerly shunned by the medical profession, some service providers are now actively seeking access to these individuals, many of whom receive Medicaid or other government benefits, which have become a lucrative form of reimbursement for hospitals and other treatment agencies. Table 8-3 presents some tips for service providers working in research settings.

To work effectively in research environments, service providers must establish a boundary between service and research information and a procedure for sharing this information. Service providers are unlikely to have the time or the inclination to sift through voluminous research data, and researchers are unlikely to do the same with service records. The most useful way to address these issues is to collaborate in the development of the project materials. For example, a standard demographic information sheet can be divided into three sections. The first section can include information relevant to both research and service (e.g., date of birth, gender, ethnicity, family composition), the second can include information related to only service needs (e.g., detailed medical history), and the third can include information related to only research needs (e.g., detailed substance abuse history). Similarly, a fact sheet in a client's chart can contain demographic, service, and research sections.

In some situations, researchers may wish to provide or facilitate treatment but not have access to the physical space required for these activities. In the present medical funding environment, researchers working with hard-to-reach and underserved populations may find that local hospitals and other treatment facilities are very interested in providing care to these populations. These agencies may be able to provide enough space for both service provision and research activities or pay rent in exchange for the

**TABLE 8-3    Top Ten Tips for Service Providers
Working in Research Settings**

1. Establish clear boundaries between research and service activities.
2. Generate a list of additional services that research participants can access.
3. Complete research instruments neatly and fully to facilitate data entry.
4. Develop a protocol for providing clinical information to researchers.
5. Describe your intervention in concrete terms.
6. Educate researchers about your intervention by providing training.
7. Provide relevant workshops for research participants (e.g., safe injecting, how to access services, employment skills).
8. Discuss findings with researchers to help them understand service implications.
9. Discuss research findings with your own clients to better understand their implications.
10. Help researchers write funding applications to continue studying your services.

opportunity to receive revenue from their services to these populations. In one NDRI project, we were interested in collecting data from participants who were HIV-positive, had children, and were not receiving family services. One aim of the project was to connect these families with services. To do this, we collaborated with the social work department at a local hospital. Our research project hired outreach staff to recruit families, and the hospital provided a social worker to deliver services. Our research project provided office space in a local storefront and trained the social worker in a brief data collection instrument. Through this collaboration, as researchers, we were able to improve our recruitment by providing intake services locally, collect data on important research questions, and establish a collaborative relationship with a local service provider. Participants benefited from their ability to access services locally, and the local hospital benefited by engaging this difficult-to-reach population.

More general activities that facilitate both research and service needs can also be provided in research settings. For researchers who have community research sites, one possibility is to present regular workshops for staff, research participants, and other community members. Attendance can be optional, and these activities do not need to be part of the formal research project. In addition to providing a valuable service, these workshops also help to improve participant retention in ongoing studies because they increase the frequency and quality of contacts between staff and participants. In the project described in the previous paragraph, which connects families in which at least one member is HIV-positive to treatment services, a regular series of workshops was provided for new outreach staff. One workshop presented an overview of HIV. Another workshop focused on employment skills, as many new outreach workers have limited work experience. Clients viewed these workshops as an additional program benefit; in fact, the employment skills workshop now serves as an ideal recruitment location for new outreach workers. Both workshops provide a tangible benefit for research participants who would otherwise have no access to this type of service.

Researchers who work with populations that may require treatment and prevention services and who elect not to provide these services themselves are ethically bound to provide referrals. In my previous example, we chose to provide a community site for social work intake to meet this obligation. In other situations, researchers choose to make referrals to services because doing so relieves the research project of the burden of providing or arranging these services directly and allows all research staff to devote their full efforts to research activities. Before research activities are started, referral lists are typically developed and distributed to all research staff. When our staff conduct street interviews for a project targeting high-risk youth, they are prepared to escort these youth to service agencies if the youth request it and to address psychiatric or medical emergencies with immediate referrals. In addition, senior staff are always available by beeper or cell phone to assist with emergencies. Although we have decided that our project is not equipped to provide street-based services directly, our referral system is designed to serve as the first step in this process.

Because many of the hard-to-reach populations described in this book need treatment but are not receiving it, many research studies specifically target these populations. These studies may seek to determine, among other things, prevalence of illness, risk behaviors, and reasons for not receiving treatment. Often participants do not wish to receive treatment because of prior negative treatment experiences or because of the perceived inaccessibility of high-quality treatment. Providing even minimal services offers an effective way to maintain contact with research participants. For example, research projects working with injection drug users have adopted outreach strategies, and researchers routinely distribute condoms, bleach kits, and personal hygiene kits, in addition to providing treatment referrals as appropriate. These services allow for increased contact, making follow-up and tracking easier for research purposes, and provide a way to address participant needs that are not addressable in a research-only context. Even if participants do not wish to receive any services, the ongoing contact provides potential opportunities to engage these individuals in services when they are ready.

## CONDUCTING RESEARCH IN SERVICE SETTINGS

In some cases, researchers may prefer to work directly in service environments. In many ways, these settings provide an ideal environment for researchers. They often serve large volumes of clients, many of whom are repeat visitors over a long period. Certain types of settings may serve the populations in which researchers are most interested. For example, methadone and needle exchange programs serve drug users, shelters provide services for homeless individuals and families, and medical clinics provide direct services for people with AIDS. By working in these service settings, researchers can gain access to the populations of interest without having to devote a lot of resources to participant recruitment. Furthermore, as part of the service provision, participants may already be providing a large amount of medical and/or psychosocial information that can serve as important research data. Table 8-4 presents some tips for researchers working in service settings.

Much of the information collected in service settings is ideal for use in research. For example, clinical charts serve as rich data instruments. In some cases, these charts may provide all the information a researcher wants; in others, additional instruments may be required. The pieces of information that are most likely to overlap are the demographic data collected about each client, including physical information, family and relationship information, employment and housing status, diagnoses, and biological test results. Much of this information is collected on standard intake forms and updated regularly in agency or practitioner records. Treatment notes and other clinical assessment instruments can also be useful to researchers. Additional information gathered by researchers could include standardized assessment measures; measures of knowledge, attitudes, and intentions; and detailed biological assessments.

**TABLE 8-4    Top Ten Tips for Researchers Working in Service Settings**

1. Do your own work. Do not rely on service staff to gather information or schedule appointments.
2. Schedule research activities so that they do not interfere with service provision.
3. Create a positive work environment. Bring in snacks or coffee, and help keep work areas clean.
4. Establish clear boundaries with participants between research activities and service provision.
5. Provide support to service staff. Listen to and validate their concerns.
6. Provide regular updates of research findings.
7. Offer to provide training on research that has been done with the population being served.
8. Meet regularly with service staff to discuss the treatment implications of your findings.
9. Invite service providers to present with you at research conferences.
10. Help service providers write funding applications that describe the data you have collected.

Many research studies use chart reviews to look retrospectively at the treatment patients have received and link aspects of this treatment to patient outcome. A unique aspect of these studies is that they capture how services were actually provided because the decision to review clinical charts is usually made after clients are served. Findings from these studies can be useful to service providers because they represent an independent assessment of treatment and outcome.

In either case, whether conducting a chart review or collecting additional information, researchers must be careful not to burden service providers with the collection or retrieval of research data. When necessary, research staff should be hired to conduct this work and trained to do so in a way that does not interfere with service provision. When completed, the results of the work should be shared with service staff via discussions, formal presentations, and written reports. Both the staff hired to collect the information and the sharing of the information itself are examples of the tangible benefits that researchers can bring to the service provider.

When researchers hire staff in service settings, these staff members should be empowered to directly negotiate the way the work will be conducted with frontline service providers. In talking with researchers who work in service settings, I have heard numerous tales of senior staff negotiating agreements for data to be shared, only to find that the data are unavailable because the frontline staff, who have daily access to the data, were not consulted on how to make this collaboration possible. Reasons for these failures include lack of space, restriction of confidential information, resistance from treatment staff, and extremely limited resources, such as computers, desks, and telephones. One project director with whom I spoke purchased cell phones for her research staff working in a drug treatment program so that they would not have to burden the treatment staff by using the few available telephones. Another project director reported that providing coffee and snacks for treatment staff helped to establish a positive working environment for his research staff as they collected data in a methadone program.

An important area that must be addressed when conducting research in service settings is the identification of research participants. In many cases, research is conducted anonymously. Participants may not be required to provide their actual names, and the names they do provide to researchers are always kept separate from the information they provide. Often, researchers do not want access to any identifying information about participants other than the actual research data. Participants typically sign consent forms that are given code numbers, and only the code numbers appear on research documents. The consent forms and documents are then stored in separate places, so that the information provided is not easily linked to individual participants. When such systems are adopted, participants provide comprehensive information to service providers while remaining anonymous to researchers. The increasing computerization of clinical information also facilitates this anonymity by easily allowing the deletion of identifying information from research databases while retaining this information in service databases.

## Client Issues

In service settings, clients often have objections to participating in research protocols. One major objection is that they report feeling like guinea pigs. These clients are uncomfortable with the experimental nature of many research protocols and are often concerned about trying treatments that have not been fully tested and approved. In addition, many people view scientific research as exploitative and abusive. Because of several infamous historical cases in which the goals of research superseded, or were antithetical to, the health of the research participants (for example, Nazi medical experiments and the Tuskegee syphilis studies), the public at large is often highly skeptical of participation in research projects. Although these concerns are valid, they often represent a larger underlying concern that the researcher is interested only in getting information from the participant and is not otherwise interested in the participant's well-being. Bea Krauss, in her chapter in this book, addresses these client concerns and illustrates how, by viewing the research questions within the context of the participant's life and community, researchers can be sensitive to clients' broader needs and try to validate and address these concerns in their work.

When participants are uncomfortable with the experimental nature of a research protocol, it is important to validate their fears and concerns and provide them with some specific information about the study and about research protocols in general. Clients who are potential research participants should be informed that modern ethical guidelines provide protection to research participants and that formal systems of ethical review are now in place throughout the United States to provide unbiased assessments of whether participants are adequately protected in research projects (see Chapter 7). In addition, participants can benefit from the knowledge that treatments or behavioral interventions that have not been fully tested follow carefully documented protocols to ensure patient safety, including close monitoring of participants in situations with any potential for physical risk, such as clinical trials of new medications. Often, when potential participants are presented with this information in a respectful manner and given an opportunity to ask questions, they are interested in participation. To make sure that potential participants understand what they are consenting to, it is useful to ask them to describe what they are going to be doing to check that they have followed the presentation of the consent process. In one of our projects, we have begun to "test" participants' understanding of the consent procedure by giving them a brief questionnaire immediately following the informed consent process. We correct any misunderstandings and clarify information as needed prior to beginning our interviews. We also administer this questionnaire before follow-up interviews to assess participants' retention of consent information. The findings from this questionnaire will enable us to improve our consent process in our future research and service projects.

Individuals who do agree to participate in research may feel that they are being asked to devote too much time to the research. Research protocols tend to be fairly lengthy, requiring interviews, assessments, and sometimes biological testing in excess of that required for satisfactory clinical treatment. In most cases, these issues can be addressed when informed consent is obtained by clearly outlining the activities that will take place as part of the research protocol. Assessing participants' level of fatigue, allowing them to take breaks when they are fatigued, and consistently providing information about the activities that will occur at each visit and how long each visit is expected to last can make participants more comfortable with their level of participation. Perhaps most important, responding to participants' complaints by using shorter instruments will provide both better data and a better experience for the participants. In our research with injection drug users, for example, we try to keep our interviews to a maximum of 30 minutes. We developed this procedure because we learned that participants in other studies were complaining about longer interviews and we noticed that our early participants became fatigued or began to suffer withdrawal symptoms when the interview protocol kept them in our field offices for longer periods.

Another common complaint is that participants receive no direct benefit from research activities. Many participants perceive that the benefits of research will not be realized until the end of a study and that the real beneficiaries are the researchers who are being paid to conduct the studies. Although research studies do ideally have long-term societal benefits, including improved and more efficient treatment, they must be designed to also provide immediate benefits for participants. These benefits, described in detail throughout this book, can include ancillary services (training, support groups), compensation for participants' time (money, food, gift certificates), and referrals for needed services (food, shelter, medical care, drug treatment).

## Staff Issues

Research staff can also face unique difficulties in service settings. Working on a daily basis in some service environments, such as detoxification or drug treatment programs, places research staff in direct contact with clinical issues in these settings. To negotiate these settings, staff must be highly trained or have extensive experience in working with these populations, thus commanding higher salaries, which puts pressure on research budgets. However, these are the type of staff needed to negotiate complex service environments. For example, one research interviewer works full-time in a detox program for opiate users. Although her job is to collect data on recent drug use, because of the setting in which she works, she is forced to handle the complex clinical issues of opiate withdrawal, confinement to a program, and possible referrals for long-term treatment. In addition, she must negotiate with program staff for time and space to interview her research participants. Her training and interpersonal skills enable her to negotiate this environment on a daily basis by treating clients and staff with respect, recognizing the issues they are facing in a detox setting, and providing support at the same time she is collecting data.

Service providers may themselves object to specific aspects of research methodology. Many research protocols require random assignment of clients to different study conditions (e.g., different treatments, different times of assessment). Random assignment is one of the most basic standards of scientific research that evaluates or compares interventions, and it is designed to ensure that any differences found are due to different interventions and not to preexisting differences in the subjects assigned to each intervention (e.g., clients who are more verbal are assigned to a counseling intervention, which then proves to be more effective than a psychoeducation intervention). In some cases, service providers may feel uncomfortable in assigning clients to a treatment they perceive as less effective or as a poor match for a particular client. However, they may feel more comfortable when they become aware of the reasons for random assignment. In the parent–child HIV prevention project described in Chapter 6, parents are randomly assigned to receive either a parent-training group or a packet of information. This assignment is made after the initial assessment is completed and requires the interviewer to open a sealed envelope to determine whether the parent will be offered training. During some interviews early in the project, the staff became aware that a participant would greatly benefit from the training. The staff approached project administrators and asked if they could assign particular parents to the training group. When the rationale for random assignment was reviewed—namely, that a proper scientific evaluation of the curriculum would allow us to determine its effectiveness and potentially disseminate it widely—staff members became more comfortable with this aspect of the study design. In this example, the staff, some of whom were community members who viewed themselves as service providers for research participants, recognized the value of random assignment in the larger mission of the project. Although this example is unique in that the "service providers" were actually research staff, the principle of clearly explaining research procedures to frontline staff applies in any setting.

The issue of access to research data is important when these data are collected in service settings. Although researchers may prefer to limit access to research data to individuals who have no contact with research participants, service providers want and need access to all information available about a given client. This conflict may manifest itself when individuals are motivated to censor the information they provide to either researchers or service providers. For example, many recovering substance abusers continue to use drugs while in treatment. A researcher wishing to understand this process may collect data at a local drug treatment facility. Participants in the research, however, may not wish to divulge their continuing drug use to their counselors or to other participants in the program. In this case, a clear boundary between research and service activities is required.

In regard to maintaining confidentiality, it is also important that participation in the research interviews does not, in and of itself, reveal the presence of ongoing drug use or other stigmatized behavior. For example, a researcher conducting street interviews with drug users must be discreet when interviewing participants because the mere presence of the interviewer may indicate to others in the vicinity that the participant uses drugs. Similarly, a researcher working with HIV-positive individuals in drug treatment may inadvertently reveal participants' HIV status by interviewing in sight of other people. To address these concerns, researchers often conduct recruitment and interviews in separate locations (e.g., recruit a participant in the park but meet in a coffee shop or field office for the interview) and maintain discretion when describing their work to nonparticipants (e.g., "I'm conducting a health study").

It may also be difficult or frustrating for service providers to follow the structure of research protocols. Structured research interviews often limit the interviewer's freedom to follow up interesting answers. (Ethnographic and qualitative interviews do, however, allow the interviewer greater latitude in pursuing interesting areas.) Research interventions tend to be highly regimented, typically intended to deliver standardized procedures in a consistent fashion across all participants. Many service providers believe that these types of interventions constrain the "art" of service provision and their ability to individualize patient care. One possible compromise is to accept enough structure to meet research requirements while allowing enough freedom to meet service requirements. For example, in an NDRI evaluation of a program that seeks to teach communication skills to high-risk youth, we have structured guidelines for number of sessions and overall content of each session, but we allow counselors to decide how to deliver that content (e.g., role play, group exercise). At the end of the project, we will have data on overall outcomes and the various methods used to achieve these outcomes.

Once projects are under way, researchers and service providers have to continue to interact. In a truly collaborative venture, information moves in both directions between researchers and service providers. Researchers can provide regular updates of their findings to service staff, and service providers can provide information to help researchers understand the data. One NDRI project evaluates drug and violence prevention programs in local school districts. For many districts, these evaluations take place over an entire school year. One option would be to collect information during the year and then submit a final report to each district. However, this option does not allow sharing information during the project. Instead, research staff meet with representatives of each school district shortly after collecting each wave of data. In this way, programs receive feedback right after the data are collected, and researchers are better able to understand the data they are collecting. This model of collaboration serves both researchers and service providers, and it facilitates their future work together by enhancing their understanding of the other's activities.

If existing data are being collected, they can be tabulated for use in applications for funding to provide continued or additional services. When this process is successful, a system develops in which the data are used to improve programs, and the collaborative process between researchers and service providers becomes routine. Because this data collection is developed through a collaboration of researchers and service providers, it is usually applicable to both research- and service-based funding applications. In one research study that included collaboration with service providers, we found that street youth rarely used HIV testing or other medical services, except when symptoms became severe enough to visit a hospital emergency room. When we presented this information to service providers, we decided to prepare a joint application for funding to help prepare street youth for HIV testing. This project, if funded, will provide research staff to collect the data and treatment staff at a local service agency to help design and carry out the intervention.

## CONCLUSION

In this chapter, I have attempted to illustrate the rationale for, and value of, collaboration between researchers and service providers who work with hard-to-reach populations. Whether this collaboration takes place in a research or service setting, establishing the structure and framework for such collaboration requires an investment of time and resources. However, integrative models of research and service delivery, such as those presented here and throughout this book, provide tangible benefits to both researchers and service providers. More important, when these models are applied to hard-to-reach populations, who typically have multiple problems and little access to services, they can engage and retain participants in important research while simultaneously providing a level of service participants are comfortable with.

## SUGGESTED READINGS

Center for Substance Abuse Treatment's Treatment Improvement Protocols Series (TIPS). Available online at www.samhsa.gov/csat, or toll-free at 1-800-729-6686. *This series of free publications provides best practice guidelines for the treatment of substance abuse. These guidelines can help both researchers and service providers understand current state-of-the-art treatments for many hard-to-reach populations.*

Grimm, L. G., & Yarnold, P. R. (1995). *Reading and understanding multivariate statistics.* Washington, DC: American Psychological Association. *Provides an easy-to-understand explanation of some of the most common statistical procedures used in research studies.*

Hayes, S. C., Barlow, D. H., & Nelson-Gray, R. O. (1998). *The scientist practitioner: Research and accountability in the age of managed care.* Boston: Allyn and Bacon. *Describes a model of research and service collaboration used by clinical psychologists and other treatment professionals.*

# AFTERWORD

Early in my research career, I would marvel at reported census data concerning the number of heroin users in New York City. The data would be presented with a large range of possible error, such as reporting between 100,000 and 300,00 heroin users in a specified area. I wondered how the data were collected. Did someone go door to door asking residents and apartment dwellers if they were heroin users and addicts? If so, what degree of accuracy could be expected? Moreover, I was leery of the quality of data collected in neighborhoods where an interviewer might be suspected of being a police informer or immigration official. Through my association with the research conducted at NDRI over the past several decades, I learned how these problems could be addressed in a systematic and scientifically defensible manner.

Over time, accessing the heroin-using population became increasingly important because it was identified as a major transmission group for HIV/AIDS, other sexually transmitted diseases, and tuberculosis. The stigma and fear associated with these diseases drove heroin users further underground and made them even more difficult to find. In addition, cuts in social service programs, deinstitutionalization of the mentally ill, the increased homeless populations in American cities, and the influx of immigrants with infectious diseases have contributed to a large population in need of multiple health and social services. The need is even more acute when providers must not only access but also retain these individuals in order to provide a full course of care, such as tuber-culosis treatment or the new HIV medication regimens.

For more than 30 years, NDRI and its people have been seeking ways to access and serve this population. This extraordinarily tal-ented and creative group of researchers and service providers have developed innovative and successful ways of accomplishing this task—not only in New York City but also around the United States and in other parts of the world. Dr. Tortu, Dr. Goldsamt, and Mr. Hamid have identified many of the NDRI people who have led the way in solving the access problem for hard-to-reach and hidden populations. This book offers what we have learned by experience, training, and analysis in this area. I am proud that NDRI staff members are making this very important contribution to the field.

Fred Streit, Ed.D.
Executive Director/CEO
National Development and Research Institutes, Inc.

# INDEX